The Alligator Dance

Other books by Brenda M. Spalding

The Green Lady Inn Mystery Series

Broken Branches
Whispers in Time
Hidden Assets
The Spell Box

Blood Orange
Honey Tree Farm
Bottle Alley

A Murder for Christmas
(short story)

The

Alligator Dance

A Dance of Death, Romance, and Murder

Written by

Award-winning Author

Brenda M. Spalding

Published by

Heritage Publishing.US
www.heritagepublishingus.com

Dedicated to all the men and woman who risk their lives to protect the environment and the animals that live there. The Florida Fish and Wildlife Conservation Commission Law Enforcement Officers are unsung heroes.

The Alligator Dance

Chapter One

The early morning mist was just beginning to rise. Heat from the approaching day blanketed the men who stealthily jumped the back fence at Manasota State Park.

Five men crossed the Florida prairie heading for the river that flowed through the park and the anomaly known as Gator Hollow, a huge water-filled circular sinkhole in the side of the Myakka River where hundreds of alligators congregated. No one knew why.

Nests along its banks held the prize the men were looking for. Each one was holding fifty to eighty eggs. The nests were hidden in the scrub brush and pine that circled the Hollow. Danger lurked in the deep murky water and under the spiny palmetto fronds.

One young man went off on his own. A college kid in need of quick cash, his gambling on fantasy football had left him in debt to some dangerous people.

The Alligator Dance

Diligently digging with his hands and fighting off the stings of fire ants and the torturous bites of the large bull ants, he uncovered the nest.

"Momma, you sure did bury these down far enough." He was head down, arms deep in the nest.

Suddenly, the world went quiet. An ominous feeling crept in through the area. A small flock of egrets hunting on the shore took flight. The birds high in the trees stopped chirping, and even the pesky bugs stopped buzzing. The hair on the back of his neck stood up as a cold chill ran up his spine. He heard the low predatory growl of momma gator. Chancing a look behind him, he watched the gator rise slowly from the dark water. The water swirling and dancing along her sides as it vibrated from the deep sound of her warning. She eased her massive body out to stand on all fours and, with one last growl from deep in her throat, charged.

Scrambling to stand and run, the young man found no traction in the sand and rough ground under his feet.

He screamed as the gator's powerful jaws clamped down on his calf, piercing skin, breaking bone. She rolled, dragging him into the murky dark water.

The young man cried—clutching at the sparse shore grass that tore away in his hands, knowing his life was over. The last thing he saw was the sun rising, coloring the sky as the water closed over his head.

The Alligator Dance

Chapter Two

The day started early at the Manasota State Park that straddled Manatee and Sarasota counties on the Florida Gulf Coast. The head ranger pulled up before the station, "Hey, Darrell, how's it going?"

"Hi there, Chief, scalp anyone today?"

Ranger Seth Grayson raised his eyebrows and shook his head. "You're lucky I'm in a good mood, or I'd have your scalp on my pole," he shot back with a smile, stepping out of his old Ford F-150. Already the early summer heat and humidity were making his brow drip with sweat.

Darrell, his one full-time ranger for the summer months, came to meet him, carrying the daily logbook for the Manasota State Park. The park attendance didn't qualify for more in the summer months. Seth had worked with

The Alligator Dance

Darrell Harris for a couple of years now and liked the easy way they worked together. Seth didn't generally take the cracks about his Seminole Indian heritage lightly; Darrell was just being Darrell. The two friends were able to converse with understanding and never overstepping the line.

During the summer months, when even the mosquitoes hide in the palmettos to avoid the heat of the day, Seth worked at the park with only one full-time and one part-time ranger. Later in the cooler winter months, they would add another couple of rangers to cope with the additional seasonal tourists. The park was a haven for bird watchers and animal and nature lovers. There were miles of hiking and horse trails. The campsites were popular with families in the winter months. Visitors could bring in their RVs and use the park's hookups, or there were a couple cabins to rent. Dedicated campers preferred the primitive campsites farther out to pitch their tents and fend for themselves.

Seth and Darrell settled at the scarred picnic table, placed under a massive oak by the crushed shell-packed parking lot. "What's in the book for today?" Seth asked, tipping his hat down to shade his eyes from the sun's glare. He was hoping for a quiet easy day.

"We have a couple of groups signed up for the tour out to Gator Hollow," Darrell said, looking at the bookings. He took off his hat and smoothed his bright copper hair. "They have to be Northerners. Locals know it's too damn

The Alligator Dance

hot in June. Either that or they're just plain nuts." He laughed. Darrell was always quick with a joke and a ready smile.

"You got that right. We don't see many locals that want to hike two miles in the summer heat. They know better," agreed Seth.

"Something else you should know," Darrell said, his laugh lines wrinkling into a frown. "The poachers have been at it again. I saw several empty nests yesterday. I called the Florida Fish and Wildlife Conservation Commission. They promised they'd send someone out."

"Thanks, Darrell. I'll be inside in a minute."

Darrell took the hint and left Seth for the air-conditioned office.

Early morning was Seth's favorite time of day. The time before the heat and humidity got too high, and the park visitors arrived. He stayed a moment, sitting at the old picnic bench under the hundred-year-old water oak. The crying egrets flying above caught his attention. Glancing up, he followed their boisterous flight across the magenta and orange sky. A couple of bats flew overhead, returning to their roost in an old sabal palm behind the station house. Their erratic hunting flight was replaced by the sure and steady flight to their home in the pine fronds—a perfect place to rest before their next evening flight. He wished it could be this peaceful all the time.

The Alligator Dance

A slight smile brightened his face as Seth remembered how his father had taken him fishing many times along the Peace River—or how they often joined his cousins to go hunting on the Big Cypress Reservation on the edge of the Everglades. These trips taught him to respect the land and the animals that lived there. It was a lesson he valued and had led him to become a park ranger.

Lately, he'd been wondering if being a park ranger was enough for him. He liked his job, educating visitors about the park and its mission to conserve the environment, but was there more he could be doing with his life? Protecting the environment and the animals that lived there had always been what he wanted to do. He needed something to change, but he didn't know what. Seth thought about taking a vacation. He made up his mind to check out one of those travel places in Sarasota the next time he was in town. Putting a little excitement in his life might be just what he needed.

Pushing up from the bench, he headed for the park office building. Entering the office, Seth took off his wide-brimmed hat and wiped the sweat that stung his gray-green eyes—a gift from some long-forgotten white ancestor. That ancestor had also passed down his height of almost six feet, unusual for a Seminole. Running his hands through his coal-black hair, he hung his hat on a peg by the door. In college, Seth styled his hair with a short back and sides and not in the

The Alligator Dance

bob favored by his more traditional relatives. It was easier for him to fit in, and he had decided to keep it that way.

The Alligator Dance

Chapter Three

Seth stood, patiently waiting for the coffee to brew, talking with Darrell. "About those poachers, wasn't Stan supposed to be checking that area?"

"Stan's new. He'll get better," Darrell said, defending the part-time ranger. Stan had only been with the park for a few weeks. "Maybe he just didn't see the empty nests when he was out on patrol."

"I know, but the poachers don't give a shit and won't wait until he learns his job. They want to make the most money in the shortest amount of time. He has to keep his eyes open," Seth said, placing a steaming cup in front of Darrell.

"Look, maybe you need to go out with him next time and show him what to look for. Being part-time, maybe he hasn't worked gator nesting season before." Seth didn't want

8

The Alligator Dance

to be the bad guy in this, but Stan had a job to do. He'd give Stan a break because he was new—for now.

"Could be, but sometimes I get the feeling that his mind is not on the job at hand. He seems to spend a lot of time on his cell phone. I'll go with him next time out." Darrell grunted, taking a sip from his mug. Darrell didn't like working with Stan. The young part-timer didn't seem to have a real interest in what being a park ranger was all about, which aggravated him. Actually, it really pissed him off.

"Look, I've been doing some research on the internet," Darrell said, blowing on his cup. "I found out poaching alligator eggs is a big problem for the ecosystem. Alligator farming is booming. The demand for hides from the fashion industry has been growing over the last few years. There is a lot of money in gators."

Darrell passed Seth some articles downloaded from the internet. "A five-foot hide could fetch around four hundred dollars, up or down depending on the market. Add in the meat, and one alligator could bring over a grand. Did you know some of those big fashion houses own gator processing plants? They're crippling the legal gator hunting and harvesting trade because they don't care where the hides come from—legal or not."

"Yeah, I heard about a new alligator farm that opened out by Arcadia or Myakka," Seth said, shuffling through the pages. "I've been meaning to check that out."

The Alligator Dance

"Right. But get this—it's fascinating stuff," Darrell said, flipping to another page. "The reptiles don't breed well in captivity, which has led to trying to get eggs in other ways. The state charges a fee for every egg collected on public land. The poachers don't like to pay the state fees. There are only thirty permits issued each year to collect eggs in the wild. That's why there is so much poaching."

Tires crunching on the crushed shell in front of the ranger station interrupted their conversation and signaled their first visitors.

"I'll go," Seth said, retrieving his hat off the peg. He brushed his hair back and slapped the hat on his head. "You deal with the Wildlife guy. I'm not in the mood."

The Alligator Dance

Chapter Four

Seth watched the first visitors step out of an older model dark blue Honda, a mom, a dad, and two rambunctious young boys.

"James, Lucas, stop that running around and come here," the mom shouted. "Can't you do anything to control your kids?" She sent a helpless look at her husband.

"They need to run around. It's the great outdoors, after all," the dad said, extending his arms, encompassing the park's surroundings.

Ignoring his wife and kids, the father extended his hand to Seth. "Hi, we're the D'Angelos. We booked a tour to Gator Hollow. The boys are excited to see the alligators. Call me, Tony. This is my wife, Gloria."

"Nice to meet all of you. We'll get started in just a bit," Seth said. He could not believe the way Mr. D'Angelo let his boys run wild. Seth felt sorry for the wife and how

The Alligator Dance

disrespected she was by her husband. It was not his place to say anything, but he sure wished he could. The park was a relatively safe place, but it was also dangerous, especially to young children not used to watching out for snakes.

. "I hope you brought plenty of water. It's a long hike."

"Gloria packed some this morning," Tony said, indicating his sad-looking petite wife.

A brand-new Jeep Cherokee pulled up, and a young couple climbed out. "Hey there," the man called to Seth. "We're from Michigan on vacation. How do you guys stand this heat?" he asked, mopping his forehead with a red handkerchief "We're the Delvins. We booked a gator tour. Are you our guide?"

Mr. Devlin walked up to Seth and shook his hand, "I'm Jerry, this is my wife, Beth." He waved back in the direction of a woman looking forlorn and rather out of place in her spanking new L.L. Bean hiking boots.

"I guess I am," Seth replied. He would have to check the log and everyone's IDs before they headed out. *And here I was hoping for a nice quiet day.*

"But…we are looking forward to seeing all these alligators. You can't visit Florida and not see the alligators, right?" he said, showing off the brand-new Nikon camera hanging around his neck. The pale white couple in their

The Alligator Dance

middle thirties looked like they had never even seen a tree, much less hiked anywhere.

Seth could have picked them out as Northern tourists anywhere from the way they were dressed. Their clothes still had the creases from the packaging, and his Bermuda shorts were a dead giveaway.

"Don't forget the bugs," Beth complained, slapping at the cloud hovering around her bare legs. "Did you remember the extra bug spray?" she said, shaking the can. "This one is almost empty."

Seth took their IDs and went back to the office to confirm the registrations. The information determined staffing and appropriations for the park. Numbers mattered even in Florida's wilderness.

Only thirty people were allowed to visit the wilderness preserve area around the Gator Hollow per day. Some visitors reserved way in advance, but the summer months were slow. Few wanted to endure the heat and the mosquitoes.

It worked out well because the alligators laid their eggs in June and July and guarded their nests fiercely. In Seth's mind, the fewer visitors to that area, the better it was for the alligators. The wilderness preserve area of Manasota State Park covered more than 7,000 acres of the total 28,000 that made up the park. The preserve limited the number of visitors each day and permitted no camping.

13

The Alligator Dance

Sitting across from Darrell, Seth jokingly asked, "How about I flip with you to see who takes this lot out today?"

"No way, Chief. I did the last bunch in May. Remember, that kid got stuck with his arm down a gopher tortoise hole?" Darrell answered quickly. "Besides, I've got all these reports to do on visitor attendance and campsite inspections." He shuffled papers pretending to be ever so busy.

"OK, but I'll remember this when the church groups have their campouts. Be prepared to have lots of calamine lotion." Seth laughed as he headed out the door. Poison ivy and poison oak seemed to grow faster when the kids were around—he thought as he reached out to grab the unsuspecting campers.

"Oh, by the way, the Florida Fish and Wildlife Conservation Commission called while you were chatting with your group. They're sending someone out this morning," Darrell said.

"Thanks, terrific. Just what I need. See you in a couple of hours." Seth braced himself as he opened the door. Today's group could be trouble. A couple of unruly kids and two city mice did not make for a pleasant hike to Gator Hollow. Now someone from the FWC added up to a rough start to his morning. Probably some stuffed shirt officer with a rule book and no sense of direction. Or some old guy who hadn't left their desk in years.

He chuckled as an image of an old geezer in shorts, black knee socks and sandals came to mind. Just what he needed to start the day off right.

The Alligator Dance

Chapter Five

Another vehicle crunched into the parking area. Seth squinted into the morning sun as a gray and black FWC patrol truck pulled into a parking spot right in front of the building, reserved for visitors. *Can anything else go wrong today?*

What stepped out was not what he had imagined. What did was a sandy-haired female officer wearing a badge with a very shapely figure, in an FWC uniform, a state-issued Glock 21 strapped to a trim waist, and black leather hiking boots. Reaching for her briefcase, she gave Seth a full moon view of her assets. *Hmmm, definitely not what I expected,* Seth mused.

Jerry Devlin also stopped to admire the view and got a slap on the arm from his wife for it.

The Alligator Dance

Mr. D'Angelo was not immune, either. His wife just rolled her eyes and shrugged. "At least I know you're still alive and interested, even though it's not in me."

Seth walked over to greet the FWC officer. "Welcome to Manasota State Park. I'm Ranger Seth Grayson," pushing up the brim of his hat to get a better look at her. He liked what he saw.

For a split-second, Seth was tongue-tied. There was something about this woman that drew him.

The officer shifted the briefcase to her left hand and reached out to shake hands. "Officer Liz Corday. You called about a suspected poaching problem?" Her manner was very official and a little uptight.

Seth was taken back a bit but collected himself and shook her hand. "Yes, it's the first for us here. Do you see a lot of poaching cases?"

"More than I'd like. I deal with all kinds of illegal poaching and animal smuggling. Seems to be a lot of that activity recently in this area. I'd like to see the empty nests. The poachers usually hit private land, and you're right. This is a first, hitting a state park."

"I'm heading out that way with some visitors right now."

"Great. It will give me a chance to see the problem firsthand."

"You might want to leave your briefcase in the car."

The Alligator Dance

"Right," she answered as she turned and tossed her case into the front seat. She opened the trunk hatch, grabbing a backpack. With her back turned to Seth, the FWC officer wondered about the head ranger. She had done some research before heading out to the park and knew he was Native American. He was the first Seminole Indian she had met, stirring her curiosity. Not bad to look at either.

"James, Lucas, leave that tree alone." Mrs. D'Angelo was frustrated with her husband for not keeping their boys in check. They were busy tearing the low-hanging branches off a young pine tree struggling to grow at the edge of the palmetto brush.

"Come on, honey. It will be fun once we get started," Jerry Devlin said to his wife. "Think of all the great pictures we can show our friends when we get home," holding up his big new camera and putting his arm around his wife's shoulder and crooning to Beth.

She shrugged him off, spraying more insect repellent on her saturated legs, mumbling, "If we live long enough. I don't think I'll have any blood left after the bugs get done with me."

Joining the group, Officer Corday tossed the pack over her shoulder, "I'm ready. Lead on, Ranger Grayson."

The Alligator Dance

Chapter Six

"Come back here, boys. Don't go too far ahead," Gloria called to James and Lucas. The youngsters were racing ahead ignoring her.

"Honey, keep up," Jerry coaxed his wife, Beth.

"I don't like this, Jerry. Why couldn't we have gone to the beach and relaxed in the sun?" Beth said after walking a half hour.

"I told you that the beach has a red tide warning. I'm not going to spend a day inhaling toxic fumes and dead fish."

"We could have hung around the pool and had those little fruity drinks with the little umbrellas in them. I wanted to go home with a Florida tan to show off to my friends," she said, sulking. She gulped from her water bottle, stowed it back in her pack, and took out her bug spray again. Beth sat down in the small plot of shade afforded by a slash pine

The Alligator Dance

along the side of the trail. She eased off one of her hiking boots, grimacing at the huge red, raw blister on her heel.

"Maybe I can help you with that," Liz said, digging in her pack. She pulled out a first aid kit. "Hold on, and I'll make that feel better in no time." Liz applied a little antiseptic and a bandage to Beth's heel. She inspected Beth's other foot and treated another growing blister.

"There. That should make walking feel much better. Hiking boots do take a while to break in." One thing was clear. Beth did not belong hiking anywhere in the great outdoors. A shopping mall was more Beth's speed. At the same time, Liz felt sorry for the young woman. She was just so out of her element here, and her husband should have known better than to bring her here. There were other ways to see the alligators than tramping through miles of preserves in the heat.

"Thanks, Officer Corday. These boots are going in the trash as soon as I get home. I've had it with the great outdoors."

Liz helped Beth to stand, handing the young woman off to Gloria. "Can you walk with her for a bit?"

"Sure, no problem," Gloria said.

"Interesting bunch you have here today," Liz said quietly to Seth—walking quickly to catch up with him.

"This is a mixed bunch. I usually like taking visitors out on hikes, especially the kids. Sometimes we have family

The Alligator Dance

groups like the D'Angelos. We run courses and programs during season that the snowbirds enjoy."

"The FWC runs some of those up in Tampa, too," Liz volunteered.

They walked silently for a bit along the dirt path through the Florida prairie following the track. They passed oak trees dripping with Spanish moss, giving way to a gradual floodplain with blackwater creeks and scrub pine. Exotics appeared from nowhere: Brazilian pepper, Australian pine, alligator weed.

The boys spotted an armadillo, another hitchhiker in the Florida environment, hurrying into the palmettos. "Boys, please leave him alone." Seth stopped the two boys from poking the creature with a stick when it rolled into a ball to protect itself.

Seth glared at Tony, who was totally ignoring his children and talking with Jerry. The two men were playing with Jerry's camera, discussing angles and focus.

Tony looked back and just shrugged his shoulders. It was evident he had no interest in his children.

It was a flat two-mile walk from the ranger station to Gator Hollow. Gloria and Beth were lagging. Jerry Devlin kept stopping to take pictures of the birds along the way. Seeing a pink roseate spoonbill flying overhead fascinated him so much, he walked straight into a tall pine tree, making the kids snicker. Liz and Seth had to hide their smiles as well.

21

The Alligator Dance

Liz couldn't help whisper, "Serves him right."

"Let's stop here and give the ladies a break. The heat is getting to them," Seth said to Liz. Even the young boys were ready to stop for a few minutes. The group found what shade they could and chugged water.

"When do we get to see the alligators?" James asked.

"Yeah, I want to see the gators," Lucas whined.

"Believe me, you will see plenty," Seth told them. Now was a good time for a little alligator education. Teaching kids was the part of park work he liked best. Educating people on what the park was and what it had to offer made the job meaningful.

"Manasota State Park is more than just looking for alligators. There are rare birds, campgrounds, and even horseback riding trails. Gator Hollow was formed long ago by a karst sinkhole."

"What's that?" asked James, the older of the boys.

"That's when the limestone underneath melts away."

"How does the ground melt away?" James couldn't get his head around that idea.

"Limestone is under the dirt and very soft and porous. Water washes it away, and the ground sinks in and creates a hole that fills with water. No one knows why the alligators gather in that hole in high numbers. It's a mystery. The sinkhole is two hundred feet across and about one hundred and thirty feet deep—maybe more."

The Alligator Dance

"Has anyone ever dived down to find out?" Lucas asked Seth.

"There have been a couple of dive teams that have tried. The water is very cloudy, and visibility is bad. They used a shark cage because of the alligators. There are some interesting videos on YouTube that you can watch."

Officer Corday joined in the conversation. "At this time of year, the alligators build nests along the banks back up in the palmettos and pines to lay their eggs. If we see a nest, we must be cautious because the momma gator will be nearby to guard it."

"I heard that they sometimes eat their young. Is that true?" Tony asked, getting a poke from Gloria.

"The male gators are cannibalistic and will eat a young hatchling. That's why the momma gators are so protective. There are some excellent books in the gift shop back at the station that will help you learn more about the park and the alligators. Coloring books too. Ranger Harris can show you after the tour," Seth said, packing his water bottle away. "So, if you are all ready, we'll go see the alligators."

Seth helped Liz up from the cushion of pine needles. A few stuck to the seat of her pants. He didn't dare brush them off and left that for her to do.

James and Lucas took off, yelling, "Yeah, alligators!"

Chapter Seven

"I wish I had half their energy," Liz said.

"Me too," Seth agreed. He cast a sidelong glance at Liz, watching the sweat drip down her throat. He followed a trickle of sweat run down between her breasts. Her khaki shirt was sticking to her back. The thought of sharing a cool shower with her slid across his mind. *Where the hell had that come from? It has been a while but not that long. Or has it?*

Seth wasn't doing much better. His uniform was sticking to him in all the wrong places, making him very uncomfortable. At Gator Hollow, there would be more shade and usually a tease of a breeze filtering through the trees.

"Mr. D'Angelo better call your boys back. We could run into alligators anytime now," Seth said. "They live all around out here and often cross the trail we're on to get from one stream to another. Besides, we don't want your kids to run across any poisonous snakes."

"You didn't say anything about snakes," Beth shouted at her husband. She stopped and stood rooted in place, shaking and looking in all directions.

Liz walked back to her and threw an arm around her shoulder. "It will be fine. Snakes are more afraid of you and can sense you coming through the vibrations in the ground. They only strike in defense when you startle them. Stick to the path, and you will be perfectly safe."

"Jerry never said there would be snakes."

"There are fifty different species of snakes here in Florida, and only six of them are poisonous. They are more afraid of you, and you will probably never even know they are anywhere around," Liz said, trying to reassure Beth.

"But what about those big python snakes?"

"There haven't been any reported around here. Don't worry. As an FWC officer, I would be one of the first to know."

Beth glared daggers at Jerry, "I'm going to stay with you if that's alright?" she asked Liz in a little-girl voice. Liz knew the young woman would be more at home, sunning herself by a hotel pool, working on her tan line than hiking here in the park.

They walked on and began to come to a spot where the path led down to the alligator hole. The tops of the pine trees swayed, and the palm fronds rustled with a slight sea breeze. Pushing through the sabal palms and sharp palmettos, Beth stopped and swatted her hair, screaming, "Get it out; get it out, something's crawling in my hair." She was frantically screaming, running in circles. The two boys were laughing, rolling on the ground.

Tony was snickering and got a swat from Gloria, "You're an ass," she hissed at her crude husband.

Jerry came up to Beth, frustrated with her antics, "What's wrong this time?"

Liz stopped Beth from flailing around, holding her hands while Seth looked in her hair. Beth was shaking like a leaf. A fat palmetto bug fell to the ground.

"It's out now, Beth. See, it was just a palmetto bug." Seth showed her the big brown beetle, about two inches long, crawling away in the grass.

"Oh, yuck, aren't you going to kill it?" Beth said through her tears.

"No, every creature has a purpose. He didn't mean to scare you." Seth said.

Beth wiped her eyes. Furious with her husband's attitude, she glared at her husband. Straightening her shoulders, she was ready to walk on.

"Are we there yet?" James pouted, kicking a stone.

The Alligator Dance

"Almost, little man. Patience is a virtue," Seth told them. "The path breaks off ahead through that narrow path through the Australian pines.

The Alligator Dance

Chapter Eight

Once through the trees, they saw the expanse of Gator Hollow spread out before them. Almost a perfect circle formed at the side of the Myakka River as it flowed southwest into Charlotte Harbor and the Gulf of Mexico.

James and Lucas raced off again, trying to be the first to see the alligators.

"Call your boys back, Mr. D'Angelo," Seth shouted. "It's not safe. The alligators are nesting and are very protective at this time of year. Remember?"

Seth knew there was only a narrow beach area separating the nesting area in the trees and scrub from the water where the alligators gathered.

"Mr. D'Angelo, if you can't control your boys, I will handcuff them to a pine tree for their safety," Liz added loudly. She was fed up and afraid that the boys could run across a momma alligator protecting her nest.

The Alligator Dance

"Ok, ok, right," Tony said, walking ahead. "James, Lucas, you need to stay with us now."

"Wow," Jerry said as they broke through the trees and stood looking over the dark brown water. The breeze they enjoyed in the trees had dropped, and the sun was relentless.

"Wow is right." Liz had never seen so many alligators in one place before. "This is a pretty unique place you have here, Ranger Grayson."

"During mating season, you can hear the males grunting and calling to attract a mate. Now in the nesting season, it's pretty quiet. In a month or so, when the hatchlings appear, you will hear them calling to momma. This place has a rhythm all its own." Liz could see Seth's love of the place shine in his eyes as he looked out over the slow-moving river and the place the alligators called home.

Gator Hollow rippled with over a hundred alligators that she could see. How many more underwater? Reptiles on the banks sunning themselves stretched ten to fifteen feet long. They were laying tail to snout. The bottomless pond echoed with bellows, roars, coughs, and purrs from the males and females gathered along its shores. Liz wrinkled her nose at the funky smell the breeze brought as it washed across the water. "Whew, the smell gets to you after a while."

"It's the heat that brings it out. You don't want to be here in late July or August." Seth laughed.

The Alligator Dance

"The boys have gone too far?" Gloria came up to Liz and Seth. "I can't see them."

James and Lucas were nowhere to be seen. Tony had a sick feeling, and Gloria was in full panic mode. "Get them back here. A damn gator could eat them."

"Oh, don't be so dramatic," Tony sneered at his wife, but he was worried at the same time.

Gloria, exhausted, dropped to the ground and broke into tears. Beth and Liz each sat down beside her.

"We'll get them. I'm sure the boys are just off exploring. They're not far," Liz assured her.

The Alligator Dance

Chapter Nine

"James, Lucas," Tony yelled. "Get back here now."

"Dad, Dad!" James called. Both boys crashed out of the trees, maybe fifty feet farther down the bank.

"Come see what we found," Lucas shouted.

Gloria looked up. "Thank God."

"Dad, you gotta come see this. It's so gross," Lucas said, taking his father's other hand.

"Mr. D'Angelo, you have to keep your boys where you can see them. It's dangerous to let them run around," Seth raised his voice, hoping Tony would get the point.

"James, Lucas, Officer Corday does carry handcuffs, and I will ask her to use them if you do not stay with the group. Do you hear me?" Seth said to the boys. He was getting fed up with them not listening, and it was dangerous for them to go off on their own. Not only were there alligators to worry about, but snakes lived in the underbrush, and their bite could seriously hurt or kill a small child.

The Alligator Dance

"Yes, sir," they both mumbled, making faces behind Seth's back.

"But you have to come," he said, ignoring the warning. "It's so gross," James said, taking hold of his father's hand, dragging him along.

"Here, let us help you," Liz said to Gloria. Liz and Beth helped her to stand and catch up with Tony and her boys.

"Not too fast and watch for gators," Seth called—exasperated with Tony for not controlling his sons. Seth knew the numbers: Only about 400 people bitten by gators in Florida since the 1940s, but three deaths by gators in the past ten years. He did not want to add to the statistics.

Most visitors to the park were not aware of how dangerous it could be. Gator attacks were rare but did happen. Seth didn't want any fatalities. A young child would be a treat for a big bull gator.

"It's right over here," James said, pushing aside spiny palmetto fronds.

"Son of a bitch," Tony said, grabbing his boys to his side.

Jerry and Seth were two steps behind and looked past Tony and his kids.

Seeing the gruesome sight on the ground, Jerry turned and barfed his breakfast in the bushes.

The Alligator Dance

"Stay here," Liz ordered, not knowing what to expect. Beth and Gloria froze, waiting. Pushing past Seth, Liz exclaimed, "Oh, crap." There in the low-lying grass near the edge of the palmetto scrub lay the bloody remains of a human arm. It had been ripped off below the elbow—leaving bone and sinew exposed.

Liz unsnapped her gun holster with one hand, just in case, and pulled out her radio. She kept her eyes moving for any signs of danger while she called her dispatcher. "I need to report a gator attack in Manasota State Park at Gator Hollow."

"Gloria, keep those kids back," Seth shouted. There was no trouble as both boys clung to their mother but strained to see around her.

Beth had her head buried in Jerry's chest. Tony was busy with Jerry's camera trying to get around Liz and Seth to take a picture of the dismembered arm.

"Tony, show some respect," Gloria yelled at her husband.

Tony mumbled and stomped away. "Damn bitch, always a buzz kill."

Liz was pacing, watching the shore and the underbrush, her hand on her gun, ready for anything. A splash in the water startled her, making her take her gun halfway out of her holster.

The Alligator Dance

"I think it's a male, sir," Liz said, scanning the water while talking to Captain Jacobs in Tampa.

"Well, there is only an arm, captain. No visible tattoos or jewelry. Yeah, I'll be here."

"My captain is going to notify the Sarasota Sheriff's Office. They'll send someone out."

Seth made a call to Darrell at the ranger station to let him know what was going on.

The Alligator Dance

Chapter Ten

"Ranger Harris is on his way to pick up our visitors. I think they've had enough excitement for the day," Seth said, walking over to Liz. "Thanks for taking care of her today," Seth nodded in Beth's direction. "The woman's not up for this kind of thing. It wasn't her idea to come on this trip."

"You got that right," Liz said, watching Beth, who was sitting there leaning against a cabbage palm softly crying, her hiking boots beside her. Gloria sat beside her, fuming. Tony and Jerry were off taking more pictures.

Seth looked concerned. The two boys were not staying with the group. "Gloria, your boys have to stay close and be ready to leave when Ranger Harris gets here."

"Ranger Grayson, I've tried. They won't listen to me. Tony lets them do whatever they want. They don't understand how dangerous it is out here."

The Alligator Dance

Seth saw the boys about fifteen yards down the shore, throwing rocks at the alligators. "Jesus, Gloria. Where the hell is Tony? You guys are their parents, for God's sake. You have to keep them close or watch them get mauled or eaten?" Seth shook his head, calling to the boys. "Stop that right now and come here."

Lucas couldn't resist throwing one more rock before following his brother.

Seth walked towards the boys. He watched with dread as a ten-foot gator edged out of the murky water with his eyes on the younger boy, Lucas.

"Lucas," Seth yelled and ran, catching the boy up in his arms, turning him away from the alligator. The gator hissed, changed course, and slid back into the deep water.

Liz watched the scene unfold. It happened so quickly. A child's life could have ended in an instant.

Seth was fuming and brought the boys to their mother. "Damn it, Gloria, young Lucas here was almost lunch for a hungry alligator. I've told you how dangerous it is to let them roam around. You and Tony need to keep an eye on them. It's irresponsible. They could both be killed by an alligator or bitten by a snake. It is not Disneyland out here, for God's sake." Seth took off his hat and ran his hand through his hair. Seth turned away, afraid to say more. He was furious and could not understand how parents ignored the danger to their children. The sooner he got this group back to the station, the better.

Gloria jumped up, grabbing her sons tight. "I'm so sorry, Ranger Grayson, Officer Corday. They will say right here until we leave."

Liz took out her handcuffs and dangled them in front of the boys. "I regret not using these on you. Since I can't trust you, boys, I'm going to keep an eye on you both until you are safely on your way back to the station."

A few moments later, the sound of a vehicle came from the trail. Pushing down the path through the trees, Ranger Darrell Harris appeared.

"Hi y'all," Darrell called.

"Guess you got the full alligator experience? More than you expected, eh?" Darrell said to the boys. The boys were excited and tried to tell him all about the arm they had found and about how Lucas almost got eaten by an alligator.

"You seem to be missing a couple, Seth," Darrell managed to say after looking around at the group.

"Gloria, Beth, where are your husbands? They knew we were leaving." Seth was frustrated and trying hard to control his temper.

"They went hunting for a few more pictures. I told Jerry not to go," Beth sniffed.

The Alligator Dance

"I'll look for them while you get the others in the truck," Seth said to Liz. He was upset with both Jerry and Tony for taking off again.

Seth slogged through the undergrowth, spotting Jerry focusing his new Nikon zoom lens while Tony showed him how to compose his shots. Jerry was backing up, trying to get a wide-angle of Gator Hollow and the alligators.

"Hey, you two, the truck is leaving now if you don't want to walk back," Seth hollered.

Tony shuffled through the pine needles and spiny palmettos to meet the ranger and called over his shoulder to his new friend, "Come on, Jerry; fun's over."

Tony looked back and didn't see Jerry. "OK, Jerry, it's not funny, we got to go."

"Hey, Ranger, Jerry's disappeared," Tony shouted. "He was right here a minute ago."

Seth jogged up to Tony. "Go join the others," he commanded. Pushing through the palmettos, Seth passed a couple of empty alligator nests. Searching further, he heard the sound of grunting and struggling. Moving cautiously, he found his missing hiker.

"Don't just stand there. Get me out of here," Jerry shouted, squirming and trying to stand. Seth had a hard time holding in a laugh at Jerry's expense.

The young man was butt down in a deep alligator nest. Seth's mind was racing. The only way Jerry could have

The Alligator Dance

ended up like that was if the nest was empty. An empty nest, this time of year, meant that poachers had cleaned it out along with the others he had passed. Seth looked around cautiously in case an angry momma gator was nearby before pulling Jerry to his feet.

"Thanks, man. Who the hell leaves a hole like that where someone can fall in? I could have broken my camera," Jerry said, brushing off his shorts and checking his beloved Nikon. "I've had about all I can take of this shit today."

Seth and Jerry walked along the path to meet up with the rest of the group for the trip back to the ranger station.

"You could have lost more than your camera if there had been eggs in there, and momma was nearby."

"Shit, that was an alligator nest?"

"Yeah, they are fairly easy to spot once you know what to look for. Gator nests are usually three to six feet wide, covered by mud, sticks, palm-fronds, grass, and moss. You are lucky that the gator nest was empty. The momma gator doesn't go far from the nest. Once the babies hatch, momma sticks around in the shallows to protect them against other alligators."

"What does she need to protect them from?"

"Remember what I said about alligators being cannibals and will eat the hatchlings if given a chance? Raccoons and snakes also like alligator eggs and will eat a hatchling if they can catch it. That arm we found is most likely what remains of the guy who was robbing a nest, and a momma gator caught him."

"I didn't even think about that. Does that kind of thing go on a lot around here?"

"Poaching is rare in the parks. There are other legal places along the river, but poachers get greedy."

When Seth, Tony, and Jerry got back to the others, the park vehicle was waiting to take them back to the ranger station. Clapping Darrell on the shoulder, Seth said, "Thanks for coming to get them, pal. I don't think our guests want to hang around."

The Alligator Dance

Chapter Eleven

Liz was talking to an officer from the Sarasota Sheriff's Office when Jerry and Seth returned to the group.

"Well, I see you found our two stragglers," Liz said, smiling. "This is Officer McNulty from the Sarasota Sheriff's Office. He's in charge of the forensics team."

"Ranger Grayson, sorry about the circumstances," McNulty said, extending his hand to shake. "My guys are suiting up and ready to start a canvas of the area."

"Officer McNulty, please have someone posted as a lookout. These gators are very protective of their territory, especially in the nesting season," Seth cautioned.

"Not a problem. I'll have a couple of young officers posted who can keep an eye out."

"Please forward anything you find to my office. We'll be working together on this to find out who this individual is and how he ended up like this," Liz said.

"I sure will, Officer Corday," McNulty told her.

The Alligator Dance

The forensics team pulled on blue Tyvek jumpsuits and white rubber boots to preserve the crime scene as they set about recovering the dismembered arm. Seth watched them and knew they would be cooking inside their suits in minutes.

"Officer McNulty, I don't want to interfere, but your guys will be dropping like flies if they wear those Tyvek suits out here. How about just gloves and boots? That should be enough, right?"

McNulty looked at his men struggling to put on the suits. He was already wiping sweat from his brow. "I guess you're right, ranger."

McNulty called out to his men to discard the suits. The men all waved thanks to Seth as they spread out to search the area.

"Let's take a walk around. I'm sure there are more empty nests around here," Seth said to Liz. He was looking forward to some alone time with Liz.

"I hope we don't find any more parts of that guy lying around," Liz countered. She had seen dead bodies before, but not many came in pieces.

Walking beside Seth, Liz cast a sidelong glance at him. Who was Seth Grayson, and did he have a significant other he went home to at night? She was interested enough to want to know more about him.

Noticing her watching him, Seth asked, "You OK?"

The Alligator Dance

"Um, fine, just thinking about that poor guy who died," Liz lied.

"Me, too." However, it was the farthest thing from Seth's mind. *I really could use a cold shower right about now.*

Pushing through the sharp palmettos of the underbrush and the tangle of the kudzu vines was hot and tiring. Sweat was stinging their eyes even with a light Gulf breeze blowing through the tops of the scrub pines.

"So, how did you end up in law enforcement with the FWC?" Seth asked. He found it interesting for a woman to want the position.

"I had a favorite uncle who was a cop. I think it was the whole uniform and gun thing that fascinated me at first. I'd listen to the stories he told of bad guys and shootouts. But it was more about how he helped the shop owner who got robbed or how he helped find a lost child. That was the sort of thing that drew me. I knew I wanted to be in law enforcement and went to college with that in mind. Most women ended up behind a desk, but I wanted to be where the action was."

"Have you arrested many bad guys?" Seth said, holding a branch from hitting her in the face.

"A few. Hunting without a license or out of season is a big part of the job. Poachers are dangerous because they have the most to lose. Not only will they get prison time, but

43

The Alligator Dance

the money they'll lose from their illegal activities—as we do as well. The FWC does so much more than people realize. We protect wildlife and the land. Catching those who pollute our water or traffic in endangered species is a priority."

"Why didn't you just go for being a cop somewhere?"

"Riding in a patrol car all day didn't enthuse me too much either."

"So, you went to college, and then what?"

"My dad was always taking us camping in the state parks, and I remembered meeting a ranger on one of those trips. He told us all about the ranger service, and it stuck in my mind. Dad was big into conservation and saving the environment and suggested I look into the Wildlife Commission. When I found out they had a law enforcement branch, it was the best of both worlds for me. I get to carry a gun, arrest bad guys, and enjoy nature. What could be better?"

They were walking along as Seth scanned ahead for alligators, gator nests, and snakes. Seth did point out some undisturbed nests with momma gators standing guard. They gave these a wide berth.

He stopped and held her arm. "Here's another empty nest."

A couple of yards farther along, he found another empty nest, then another. "I bet they were here this morning.

The Alligator Dance

The dirt is still damp. Come on. Let's see how many they hit."

Seth counted ten more empty nests. "Shit, these guys are organized. And there is more than one of them." He knelt and pointed out several different boot impressions in the sandy soil.

"I think they went this way. See how they trampled the grass and scrub," Seth said, walking, head down, following the tracks.

"How many eggs you figure they stole?" Seth asked as they walked along.

"Well, at thirty eggs a nest on the low end, they took maybe six hundred eggs. Some nests can have ninety eggs in them, at an average of seventy eggs per time. We've seen about twenty empty nests today. That's what? One thousand four hundred eggs or more," Liz said. "I know that some may not hatch, and some of those that do survive may not live to adults, but that's cutting the rate that could grow and reproduce down a hell of a lot."

Seth whistled. "Damn, that's a lot of eggs. I mean, someone is messing with the natural order of things. Those eggs will not have a chance to grow and reproduce more alligators in the wild."

"That's right." Liz agreed. "My bet is they drop off four or five men, let them work for an hour or two, and then pick them up. At this rate, there will not be a single hatchling in the whole park," Liz said. "Let's go back. I'll radio in what we found."

"Then what?" Seth was impressed she knew so much about how the poachers operated.

"Maybe I can check with my office to see if there are more related poaching reports in the region: other arrests, BOLOs, that kind of stuff. I'll make a report and see what we can do to track down whoever is doing this," Liz said.

They took a slightly different route back, passing scrub pines and hearing the call of the endangered scrub-jay scolding the squirrels out hunting for pinecones. They followed the path the raiders must have taken. The dry prairie grass was trodden down by the passing of several pairs of feet, leaving an easy track to follow. The sky was crystal blue. Brown vultures circled high overhead, riding the warm thermals. It was so quiet they could hear small creatures scurrying in the underbrush as they passed. Liz tapped Seth's shoulder and pointed out a woodpecker tapping away on a tall Southern pine tree.

"Liz, see here," Seth said, coming to an open nest with a dozen eggs in it. "I'm betting this is where our poacher met momma gator. See the drag marks and a blood trail to the water."

Liz squatted down. "I think you're right. The gator surprised him and dragged him in to drown him. Gators like to drown their prey, stuff them under a log or in a depression

The Alligator Dance

in the bank and come back from time to time to snack as the body decomposes. Could be there was a fight with another alligator over her prize, and that's why the arm was torn off."

"If the alligator killed him while he was robbing the nest, where are the tray and the eggs he was stealing?"

"Someone came here and cleaned up. You can tell by the footprints, and there is a spot where his tray would have been." Seth took a stick and outlined the footprints and where the tray had been.

"Let's get back," Seth said, helping her stand. They stood facing each other. He was still holding her hand and in no hurry to let it go.

"Ah... can I have my hand back?" Liz asked.

"Sure, let's go." As Seth stepped off, he heard a crunch underfoot. Bending down, he picked up a pair of sunglasses. "I wonder if these belonged to our victim?"

"It's quite possible," Liz said. Dropping her pack on the ground, she put her hand in and came up with an evidence bag. "Never leave home without them."

Seth dropped the glasses in the bag. Liz carefully sealed the bag and stowed it away for analysis by the forensic team later. "Forensics might get some DNA off these."

They headed out again with Liz leading the way, but after a few steps, she stumbled and tripped. Seth caught her, saving her from a nasty fall. Standing there with Liz in his arms, he was reluctant to let her go.

The Alligator Dance

"You catch your foot on a root?"

"No, it felt more like a large rock," Liz kicked around in the brush, looking for what tripped her.

"Could be a gopher tortoise."

"I don't think so," she replied, slowly moving the brush with her foot. The object rolled out in front of them. Moving it around with the toe of her boot, she cringed at what she saw.

"Oh, yuck." She turned her face back into Seth's sweat-soaked chest.

There, in the sandy soil, lay the bloody head of the poacher: his eyes frozen wide and his mouth formed in a silent scream. Disturbed flies crawled from the open mouth, buzzing around to deposit their eggs on the new food source.

"The forensics team needs to expand the search. I'll call Officer McNulty. There may be more of this poor guy around," Liz said.

The Alligator Dance

Chapter Twelve

Back at the ranger station, Darrell finished up his paperwork and headed out the door. Seth settled down in one of the old office chairs, leaned back and propped his boots up on the desk. Liz sat in a chair beside one of the old filing cabinets, weary and ready to crash for the day.

"The park is open for another couple of hours. We only have a couple of overnight campers to check on," Seth said. "Stan can do that. I'll let him know. Then we can head out."

Liz leaned against the file cabinet, "I'm going to stay here tonight and take a walk around those empty nests in the morning. The forensic team will be back in the morning to take another look around too. They will have to check out where we found the head. I'll hand them the sunglasses we found, too," Liz said, pouring herself a cup of stale coffee. She made a mental note to add some bottles of iced tea to their meager supplies if she was going to be hanging around much longer.

"I've got my camping gear in my truck," she said as she walked over to a map pinned to the wall. "Can you tell me a good place where I can pitch my tent?"

"Don't you want to get a hotel room or something?" Seth asked

"I don't mind a cabin if you have one."

"The cabins are all closed up for the summer. You would be hotter than hell in one of those." Seth stopped for a moment, watching her. "Why don't you come home with me? I've got hot water, air conditioning, a hot meal, and a spare room. It's just up Myakka Trail Road. You could be back here before daybreak." *It's been a while since I've had some female company.* He dropped his feet to the floor and risked a hopeful smile. "Trust me. I'll behave."

"You had me at hot water and AC."

Seth grinned at the way her cheeks dimpled when she smiled.

Chapter Thirteen

Stan stood at the office door and knocked softly, "Hey, Seth. Hello, Officer… ma'am? Stan was curious about why a Florida Fish and Wildlife Conservation Officer was showing up at the park. Hoping it wasn't for the reason he thought.

"Stan, come on in here. Officer Liz Corday is here from the Florida Fish and Wildlife Conservation Commission. A lot has happened to brief you on, and Liz and I are getting ready to head out." Seth briefed Stan about the dead poacher and the two occupied campsites.

"Should I close off that section of the park?" Stan asked. "We don't want anyone getting into trouble out there with these poachers." Stan didn't want any more visitors discovering what was going on out at Gator Hole.

"I don't think the poachers will be back anytime soon. Especially after losing one of their crew," Liz said.

The Alligator Dance

"I'll ask my captain tomorrow when he expects the forensic crew to release the scene."

"Thankfully, we don't have any tours scheduled to hike out that way," Seth said.

"So, I shouldn't accept any more tours until the FWC gives us clearance?" Stan said.

"Do what you can to discourage any tours out that way. I don't think there will be many, but you never know. Blame it on the summer heat for now. Tell them it's too hot for hiking out there right now," Liz said. "We don't want to raise any alarms just yet. We don't want to broadcast that there has been an alligator attack either. The newspapers would have a field day."

"Hey, Julie is planning a barbecue on the weekend. Do you want to come? You too, if you're still around, Officer Corday," Stan said.

"We'll see. I'll let you know," Seth replied.

"Let me know so I can tell Julie how many," he called, watching Seth and Liz heading back out the door. As soon as they left, Stan picked up his cell phone and punched in a number.

The Alligator Dance

Chapter Fourteen

Liz followed Seth to his place in her FWC vehicle. His road passed a couple of small houses with barns and horses in railed pastures. Kids played in the front yards as the sunset over the palms and old oak trees dripping with moss that lined the dirt track. Liz followed him into the yard and pulled up beside his truck. A wide back porch overlooked an open view of the river ambling past. A monstrous shape hurtled off the porch toward them. Liz looked out from a safe position standing behind Seth.

"Hi there, did you miss me?" Seth said, scratching a big dog behind his ears. "This is Nokosi. I got him as a puppy, and he just kept growing. I take him with me when I can."

"That's an interesting name, Nokosi," Liz said, bending down to pat the friendly animal.

The Alligator Dance

"It's Seminole for dog," Seth said. "Can also mean bear."

"He's big enough to be a bear." Liz laughed.

"Wait till you see him eat," Seth joked, walking up the porch steps.

Liz took in the small, single-story farmhouse. Baskets of trailing flowers hung from the rafters of the porch, adding bright colors to the soft green of the house with butter yellow trim. A couple of rocking chairs guarded one side of the front door, and a porch swing beckoned on the other side. She imagined how nice it would be to sit there, swinging in the evening, listening to the quiet, and enjoying a glass of wine in the cooler evenings.

Entering the house, Liz saw the kitchen on the left and a cozy sitting room on the right with a fireplace for the cooler winter evenings. She dropped her bag by the door and admired the tidy little home. "Wow, do you have a housekeeper?"

"Not what you expected, eh?" Seth asked.

"I was expecting more of a man cave, dirty laundry on the floor, and a sink full of dishes and a week-old garbage stink."

She explored the sitting room, running her hand over the Indian blankets on the sofa and the comfy chairs. Colorful and exciting Indian art decorated the walls and bookshelves.

The Alligator Dance

"My aunt made the blankets for me. She uses a handloom and sells some of her blankets to the tourists."

Wandering over to the fireplace, she picked up a photo. "Your parents?" she asked, holding a picture of two older people in Native Indian dress.

"Yeah, that's my mom and dad. They were at a gathering a couple of years ago. I think one of the cousins got married. I have quite a few cousins."

He took two steaks out of the fridge, a couple of large potatoes, and a bag of prepared salad. "The shower is down that hall—towels in the closet. We can eat in about half an hour if that works for you? You aren't a vegetarian, are you?"

"I love steak. Medium rare?"

"Perfect. Take your shower. Dinner will be right along."

Picking up her bag, Liz headed down the hall.

Seth fired up a gas grill on the back porch and threw the potatoes into the microwave. He took time to feed Nokosi and refilled the dog's water bowl. Then he set to making up a quick oil and vinegar dressing.

Seth was putting the plates down on the table when Liz came from the back, wearing a pair of gray sweatpants and a pink tee-shirt, rubbing her hair with a towel. It was a wet mess, and he thought it was perfect. He also noticed she was not wearing a bra, giving himself a mental slap for noticing. *Oh, shit. It has been too long.*

Liz cocked her head, looking at Seth. "It smells great. My dad only knew how to cook one thing, blueberry pancakes, but they were the best. My mom taught Sunday school, so it was a special dad and me time."

"I like to cook. Besides, I can make something in less time than going to town takes," Seth replied, tossing the salad in a bowl. "My mother taught me to cook while I was growing up. We cooked what we hunted, deer, rabbit, even alligator. When we visited my cousins on Big Cypress Reservation near the Everglades, we would have a big feast on what the hunters brought back that day. My Uncle Zackary made a mean Seminole Gold Barbecue sauce. I put that stuff on everything." Seth laughed at the memory.

"I like barbecue, but not too hot."

"I had to cook for myself in college too. Sharing an apartment with a couple of guys who lived on takeout and pasta was doing me in. I couldn't live on the crap they were eating. I bought a couple of cookbooks and went from there."

"Same here—except I was rooming with a vegetarian. Yuck."

"Growing up on the reservation, my mom had a small vegetable garden, and we always had fresh vegetables. She grew tomatoes, lettuce—the regular salad stuff. In the summer, we had squash, peas, beans too. I still try to eat right. Native Americans can have a lot of health problems if we don't take care of ourselves," Seth told her.

"You said medium-rare, right?" Seth said, opening a bottle of red wine and pouring it into their glasses.

The Alligator Dance

Chapter Fifteen

"Not much company out here. The wine was a gift from a friend a couple of years ago. I'm not much of a drinker, and I don't like to drink alone. Once in a while, I'll have a beer and sit on the porch with Nokosi. I tell him all about my day, and he lays there and listens. Sometimes he tries to catch Cokfi, the trickster, a rabbit. But Nokosi is always outsmarted."

"I can see that." She laughed at the dog, snoring happily at Seth's feet. "Aged wine. Cool!" She took a bite of the steak. "Wow, this is good. I didn't realize how hungry I was." Liz forked salad into her mouth.

"Thanks." Seth floundered for words. He liked being alone at home and most of the time at the park, too, and was comfortable in the world he had created. It surprised him how much he suddenly enjoyed having Liz there. "Sorry, I don't usually talk this much. It's usually just Nokosi and me."

"I'm glad I decided to take you up on your offer. After hiking all day, it's nice to relax," Liz said, sipping her wine.

"I'm enjoying having the company." They sat lost in their thoughts until Seth broke the silence. "How do we go about catching these poachers?" It was time to get back to the real world.

"I want to go back to Gator Hollow tomorrow and backtrack to where the poachers came into the park. Knowing what kind of vehicle they're in, we might locate any recording video cameras on the roads leading in."

"I don't think you'll find any cameras until you get up to Tamiami Trail or I-75," Seth said. "I can help with any tracking. I used to play tracking games with my uncles and cousins on the rez. We got pretty good at it. That's how we learned to hunt as kids."

"We'll start with the empty nests and work from there." Liz shook her head—as if rearranging her thoughts. "There are more questions to answer. Where do they sell the eggs? And I need to find out if the Sarasota Coroner identified our dead guy. That might lead to who hired him.

The Alligator Dance

Chapter Sixteen

"What part of being an FWC officer do you like the best?" Seth asked Liz as he sipped the last of the wine. He thought about opening another bottle but didn't think that would be a good idea.

"I like the investigation part of my job. You just never know what you might find." She finished the last of her steak, licking the grease off her top lip.

Liz didn't know what that little motion did to Seth. He had to keep his mind focused. He had only just met the woman.

"Can I help you with the dishes?" Liz asked.

"Sure, but I want to know more about this business with the selling of gator eggs," Seth said. They worked side-by-side washing up and putting the supper things away.

"How did you become a park ranger?"

The Alligator Dance

"Gushing millions of dollars a day from the Seminole Hard Rock Casino in Tampa, all the members of the tribe who want to attend college are fully covered. I earned a scholarship to USF, graduating with a degree in environmental science. I love wildlife and the outdoors park," Seth told her.

"What about you? Did you get much resistance from your male counterparts in the FWC?"

"I did at first. The men pulled little practical jokes on me."

"Like what?"

"One time, they put a rat snake in my locker. I guess the guys expected me to scream and run. Boy, were they wrong," Liz laughed. "I picked it up and carried it outside and released it. The jokers stood around in stunned silence. No more snakes in my locker after that."

"Did they still give you a hard time?"

"A bit. Some jerks didn't think a woman could do the job until I caught my first real felon—a hunter who was determined to avoid arrest. I was more determined to cuff him. I won in the end. I wore the black eye he gave me with pride."

"A black eye. Really?" Seth smiled and shook his head. "What did he look like?"

The Alligator Dance

"A lot worse than me when they hauled him off the ground," she grinned. "Yeah, the male officers never gave me any trouble after that."

The Alligator Dance

Chapter Seventeen

The kitchen clean, Liz and Seth moved to the sitting area. Liz curled up on the sofa, tucking her feet under her. "You have a cozy place here. I love the Native American touches."

"Thanks. Nokosi and I like it."

Seth chose an overstuffed chair and swung his leg over the arm.

"I hope I'm not putting you out."

"It's fine, Liz. I like having you here."

"My place in Tampa is a new condo development. It's more a place to hang my clothes than a home. I'd rather be outside in the woods."

"I can understand that."

He felt at ease having Liz in his house. Was he reading more into her being here than there was, or was it

The Alligator Dance

wishful thinking? *Oh boy, I'm in big trouble*, he thought as he absently scratched Nokosi behind the ears. He decided to return to business. It was a safe subject.

"OK, tell me more about this gator egg poaching," Seth said, settling back with his glass of wine. "I know poachers steal and kill for profit, but why steal gator eggs?"

"Believe it or not, it's the fashion industry that drives the poaching. The hides have a value of about $50 a foot. They sell the hides to the big French fashion houses."

"Can they make all that much from alligator hides?"

"The prices go up and down a bit, but the average gator hide can fetch almost $395 to an alligator harvester. Like fashion hemlines, gator hides climb and ebb, from $50 a foot to $70. The big dog in all this is Louisiana. Their sales are four to five times that of Florida farmers," Liz said.

"So why steal Florida gator eggs? Don't they have gators over there?" Seth asked.

"They have gators, but the problem is that gators don't nest well in captivity. Louisiana uses the gator eggs to grow the gators to supply the demand for hides."

"I had no idea. I need to do a bit of research on this myself. I'll go with you tomorrow. I don't want you out there alone if there are poachers in the area."

Nokosi stood when Seth did and headed for the door. "Make it quick. I'm tired," he said.

The Alligator Dance

Liz stood too, yawning. "I really should be getting to sleep. We have an early start in the morning. Which room is mine?"

"You can have the guest room on the left. Mine is on the right," Seth said to Liz as he watched her yawn and stretch, pulling the thin fabric of her shirt tight across her chest.

Aw, shit. Seth was having those thoughts again. It had been a long time since he had had a steady relationship. Was he ready, and was Liz the one?

"Earth to Seth," Liz broke in.

"Yeah...sorry," Seth answered. "I got lost in my thoughts. We do have a busy day tomorrow. I was making a mental list of what to do. We can take Nokosi with us. He'll enjoy the change of scenery." Seth got out a special vest and lead for Nokosi. Dogs were not normally let loose in a state park. Nokosi could be off his leash for a bit until they reached Gator Hollow. After that, it would be too dangerous.

They walked down the hall together with Nokosi trailing behind. They stopped at the doors—unsure of their emotions racing about.

"Well, goodnight," Liz said, breaking the silence. "I appreciate you letting me stay." She opened her door, walked in, and, looking back at him, closed it for the night. She leaned against the door. What would it be like if she had

65

invited him in? Should she have invited him in? *No, you idiot. You just met him.*

Seth undressed quickly and slid into bed. Nokosi curled up on the floor, a soft snore soon drifting up.

Seth was not as lucky. Thoughts of Liz sleeping across the hall haunted him. He lifted his blanket. "Down, boy. Maybe another time." He cursed his overactive imagination, turned over, and tried to sleep.

Across the hall, Liz's thoughts were keeping her awake, too. She longed to fall asleep with someone's arms wrapped around her. But she was not the kind of person who jumped from bed to bed. Only love and trust could win her heart and a place in her bed.

The Alligator Dance

Chapter Eighteen

Liz woke in the dark and fumbled to read the time on her phone. "Christ, it's only five," she muttered, stretching and rubbing the sleep from her eyes. She padded across the hall, visited the bathroom, and followed the smell of fresh-brewed coffee to the kitchen.

"Hey, sleepyhead," Seth said when Liz walked in. He poured waffle batter into the hot waffle maker. "Grab a cup. Waffles will be ready in a minute."

Liz got her coffee and sat, observing Seth. Watching his muscular back and narrow hips, hair wet from a shower, like a raven's wing caressing his neck. She wondered what kind of man he was—a Native American living in a white man's world, working for the Florida Park Service. A man who valued nature, loved his dog, kept a tidy house, and could cook. What more could a woman want?

The Alligator Dance

But what did she want? She had been awake most of the night wondering, thinking. Most of her relationships had been brief, lasting only a few weeks or months, except for her last relationship, which had ended in disaster. She wanted more. Liz wanted the whole package, husband, children—and yes, even the stupid white picket fence.

She cringed at the thought. She would remain true to herself, her own person, and no one was going to change who she was and what she wanted to be. Yet, this man was like no other. Seth had set her thinking about what might be if she dared.

"Uh, Liz," Seth said—laying her breakfast before her.

"Oh, thanks." Liz made a quick recovery, picked up her fork, and took a bite. "Oooh, heaven." Set in front of her was a plate with bacon, a glass of fresh orange juice, and a stunning Indian design centerpiece. The vase was authentic Seminole pottery filled with bright yellow sunflowers. She had seen the flowers growing in front of Seth's porch. He had so many facets to him, waiting for her to explore. Seth was, by far, the most intriguing man she had ever met.

"We need to eat and get going. The sun will be up about six, and we'll have light to track at seven." He finished his plate and took it to the sink. Nokosi bumped her leg and looked up at her with sad, pleading eyes.

The Alligator Dance

"Don't you dare give in to him. He's a big mooch, always begging for bacon. I guess he figures you don't know the rules about not feeding beggars," he laughed—looking at the dog, pleading.

The dog's eyes followed Liz's plate when Seth took it away to the sink. Giving up on getting a treat, the big dog ambled to his bowl and gobbled his breakfast.

"Nokosi will finish by the time we get ready to leave," Seth said. "Do you want to leave your things here and come back for them?"

"No, I'll throw my gear in my vehicle and follow you back to the park. I'll leave for Tampa from there."

She hoped that he would want her to come back. Liz wanted as much time with him as possible and liked being in his house. It felt right somehow.

The Alligator Dance

Chapter Nineteen

When they got to the park, Darrell walked out to greet Seth, while Liz found a place to park in the shade.

The big dog greeted Darrell, almost knocking him down. Nokosi's whole body was shaking with excitement from his nose to his tail. "Whoa there, Nokosi, nice to see you too," the ranger said, struggling to stay standing. The dog finally romped away to explore the nearest palm tree and leave his mark. "You want to leave him with me while you check out Gator Hollow?" Darrell asked. "I don't mind. We're good pals."

"Nah, he can tag along."

Darrell bumped Seth on purpose and jerked his head in Liz's direction.

"You two a thing now?"

"Jesus, Darrell, I just met her. Get your mind out of the gutter." Seth shook his head at the insinuation.

The Alligator Dance

"Any updates we should know about?" Seth asked when Liz joined them. "Liz and I are taking another look around Gator Hollow this morning."

"We have some overnight campers scheduled for the weekend. It's getting too hot for most people," Darrell said, leading them into the air-conditioned office.

Seth leaned against the old file cabinet, letting Liz have one of the chairs.

"Well, try to keep an eye on Stan. Maybe go on patrol with him a couple times—especially to the more remote parts of the park. He needs more training if he hopes to come on full-time."

"We better get moving." Seth put on his wide-brimmed, sweat-ringed Stetson. Liz picked up her pack. Seth tried to take it from her and hefted it on his shoulder.

Liz grabbed her pack from him and shoved it on her back. "Please don't treat me like a girl. I can carry my own pack." She had fought long and hard to be accepted as an FWC officer, equal to any other officers. No man was going to make her feel she was not up to her job, even if it meant carrying a thirty-pound pack.

"I know you can. You can carry it back, OK?" Seth knew that it would be lighter coming back because they would drink some of the water. Besides, his mother raised a gentleman.

The Alligator Dance

Liz gave up with a shrug. "Not worth fighting over," she mumbled, pushing past him.

Darrell raised his brows. "Not a good way to start the day, Chief," he warned.

"You're right. I should have asked. Guess it was a bit sexist. But, after a two-mile walk to Gator Hollow, she'll be thanking me," Seth said. "Come on, Nokosi. Time to catch some poachers."

Seth jogged to catch up with Liz. "Hey, what's the rush? It's a long walk in the heat. Better slow it down."

"I'm fine," she grumbled. "I don't like being treated special because I'm a woman."

"I'm sharing the load, that's all."

"Right. I'm sorry, thanks," Liz said. "Look, it's a nice day, not too hot yet. We have a ways to go. Let's try and enjoy the walk." The sun was just starting to peek over the eastern horizon casting the sky with purple color. The trail ahead was still dark, but creatures were stirring and chirping in the trees and palmetto scrub.

They walked in silence for the first mile. Nokosi ranged on ahead and then strolled back to check. Seth pointed out a couple of scrub-jays nesting in the rugged Florida dry prairie. "Hear that scolding? They growl, too," he said.

"I never thought of Florida as having a prairie until I worked for the FWC," Liz said.

The Alligator Dance

"This is the Myakka dry prairie. There are also dry prairies around the Kissimmee River and one that extends from Lake Okeechobee to Osceola County. Not many know about these prairies. Everyone thinks Florida is all beaches and swamps."

Liz stopped short and grabbed Seth's arm. "Look, a couple of sandhill cranes," she whispered. There in the middle of the track ahead stood two cranes about three feet tall.

"The Indians call them iron head cranes because the red on their heads looks like rusted iron," Seth said. They walked on slowly so as not to frighten the birds. The cranes watched them approaching and smugly turned and strolled unconcerned back into the saw palmettos and the slash pines of the prairie.

Seth called Nokosi back and put the leash on him. Moving carefully through the thick, dense plant-covered edge of the riverbank, they smelled the Gator Hollow before they spotted it. Alligators lined the banks. Some big bulls were fifteen feet. The smell in the rising heat was foul. They could almost taste the green stench of the water and didn't even want to think of the underlying flavors. The place was a step back in time.

The Alligator Dance

Chapter Twenty

"Let's start where we found the empty nest and the blood trail," Seth said, leading the way. Seth cast around for any signs or tracks that the poachers left behind or raided nests they missed yesterday. He squatted down to prod something in the sand. Liz tried to see what he was looking at.

Seth stood up and looked to the west. "They came in that way," he said, pointing with his chin. "Nokosi, come," he called and strode off. Liz jogged to keep up with his long-legged frame. She had to admit the view of his broad shoulders and trim waist did things to her insides she'd not felt in a very long time.

"Hey, remember me," she called as he pulled ahead. She had to stop, resting her hand on her knees.

"Can I have some of that water?" she puffed.

The Alligator Dance

Seth came back. "It's OK," he said, handing her the water. "It's the heat and humidity that gets to you."

"It's not that; it's your pace. Those long legs of yours are making me double-time it."

After a few minutes of rest, they headed off again. Pushing through the scrub pine and undergrowth, following footprints and broken branches left by the poachers, they came to the trail again. The track Seth was following crossed the trail and continued across the prairie.

"I know where they came in," Seth announced after walking a half-hour. "These criminals didn't follow the trail. They cut across here," Seth said, pointing across the prairie with his chin. "If we keep going, we'll come to a road that runs along the south boundary of the park. That's likely where they jumped the fence and came into the park."

"Let's go back to the station," Seth said. Liz was dripping with sweat. Shirt, khakis, hat soaked through, dark stains were running down her back.

"We can take it slow going back," he said. "The heat and humidity are rising, and we don't want to get heat exhaustion." He'd slow down for her sake but didn't want her to know it.

"I hope they've found out who the arm and head belong to," Liz said as they walked. "We can call the lab back at the station. Who the hell hired that poor guy and didn't seem to care that he ended up dead?"

Chapter Twenty-one

Arriving back at the ranger station, Liz and Seth saw Darrell talking to three young men at a picnic bench under a big oak tree.

Darrell waved for Liz and Seth to join them. "Hey, you two, how was the hike?" Darrell knew better than to broadcast that there had been bits of a body found at Gator Hollow.

"We found out a couple of things," Seth said. "I'll tell you later."

"Hi guys, welcome to Manasota River Park," Seth said, greeting the visitors.

One of the men stood up and extended his hand, "Hi, I'm Jeff Conroy. My friends here are Joe Paloma and Mike

The Alligator Dance

Harshaw. We're visiting my folks in Bradenton from New York. We're attending Columbia University up there."

Seth shook hands and introduced Liz. "This is Officer Liz Corday from the Florida Fish and Wildlife Conservation Commission. What brings you to the park today?"

"We were sitting around, and my dad was talking about how he used to bring my sister and me to this park when we were kids," Jeff explained. "I thought it might be fun to come out and explore a little. I wanted to show my friends here some alligators. Joe is a native New Yorker. Mike is from Washington State. They've never seen alligators in the wild before."

"They saw a brochure that mentioned the park and Gator Hollow," Darrell told Seth and Liz.

Seth and Liz looked at each other, knowing what was coming next and dreading it.

"Yeah, my dad had one lying around and showed it to us," Jeff explained.

"Yeah, that sounds like the place we are looking for," Mike piped up. The three probably in their early twenties. All were good-looking and built like jocks. Joe was dark with the swarthy complexion of his Italian heritage. He had the thick New York Bronx singsong. Mike was taller than the others and didn't say much.

"How do we get to this Gator Hollow?" Jeff asked.

The Alligator Dance

Seth wished that they had not asked about Gator Hollow just now when there were poachers lurking and body pieces strewn along the shore—not to mention nesting season.

Darrell spoke up before Seth could stop him. "You have to sign up for it. It's a two-mile hike down the trail and then follow the signs. It's best to go in the early morning before it gets too hot and humidity gets bad."

"What do you think, guys? You up for it?" Jeff asked.

"Sure, why not," Mike and Joe agreed.

"Can we sign up for tomorrow morning?" Joe said. "We only have a couple of days left of our vacation. We've got summer jobs to get back to. We'll need to bring water and other stuff." Joe was always the voice of reason. He was the oldest of five kids and expected to lead the way for the rest of his brothers and sisters.

Liz had been listening. "Y'all sure you don't want to wait a while until the winter months?" She could demand that the park close the trail to Gator Hollow, but she would have to write a report, and the word might get out. They had a better chance of catching the bad guys if the perps didn't see law enforcement coming.

"It's very hot and humid this time of year. Are you sure you are up for it?" Liz asked.

"A little heat won't bother us, will it, fellas?" Mike spoke up.

The Alligator Dance

"Yeah, an extra bottle of water or two and will be fine," Joe countered.

The young visitors would not be put off. Liz and Seth both tried, telling them about heat exhaustion and the humidity and the bugs. It didn't matter. They made plans to be at the park when it opened at eight the next morning. Seth would send Stan out early to check out the area. It wouldn't do to have anyone else end up on the alligators' menu.

The Alligator Dance

Chapter Twenty-two

The three college kids were waiting when Darrell unlocked the gates. They drove in slowly and parked in front of the ranger station.

Getting out of their car, Jeff asked, "Where's that other guy and the wildlife lady? She was kinda hot. Great figure, sandy-blond hair, long legs." Jeff smirked and smacked his lips. "I thought they'd be coming with us today." Jeff was the worrier, yet he didn't want to let on.

"Seth and Officer Corday have other business today," Darrell countered. "The trail is clearly marked and cell phone reception is a bit iffy, but you'll be fine. Beware of snakes. Don't go near the alligator nests. You don't want to tangle with a momma gator protecting her eggs."

"OK, then let's start walking," Joe said, eager to get going. He dumped three backpacks from the back of their rental convertible.

The Alligator Dance

"You guys got plenty of water?" Darrell asked. "It's going to get hotter than hell in a couple of hours."

"Yeah, I packed three bottles for each of us and some power bars," Joe answered, throwing a pack at the feet of each of his friends. "And a small first aid kit just in case."

Jeff chuckled. "Joe's our mother hen. He's always looking out for us." Jeff clapped Joe on the shoulder and picked up his pack. "Let's go, men."

Mike cussed and picked up his pack and followed the others through the gate and down the Gator Hollow trail. Darrell was not worried about the group so long as they used their heads.

The Alligator Dance

Chapter Twenty-three

Liz had agreed once more to stay at Seth's to allow an early start—as they both wanted to go to the medical examiner's office in Sarasota to see if anyone had identified the body—or the parts—they had found. If they could ID who the dead man was, they would have their first lead to the egg thieves.

Nokosi woke Seth, nudging his arm until he got up and let him out. Seth knocked on Liz's door to wake her up. She opened her door and showed him she was up and on the phone.

Already sitting at the kitchen table, Seth had his hands wrapped around his coffee cup when Liz walked into the kitchen after hanging up the phone. Seth asked, "Was that the coroner's office? What did they say?"

"Yes. We don't need to go to Sarasota today. They ran the prints from the hand on that arm," Liz said. "He is—

The Alligator Dance

or was—a college kid, Landon March. He went to USF at the Sarasota-Manatee campus. You fancy a ride out there to do a bit of snooping? Maybe find out who hired him to raid the nests?"

"Why not," Seth said, gathering up the breakfast dishes.

"You know," Liz began leaning back in her chair. "I could get used to you fixing me breakfast every morning." Blushing, she suddenly realized what she had implied—the color rising in her cheeks. Flustered, she dumped her coffee in the sink and rushed out of the room.

Seth leaned against the sink and watched her leave. He had been wondering the same thing. Bending down to scratch Nokosi behind the ears, Seth murmured to the dog, "Maybe we have been alone for too long, my friend." His gray-green eyes looked to a future that might be. *Did he want it? Or did he want to continue as he was?* Suddenly, he wanted to see his parents. He needed their wise counsel. He had not visited them in a couple of months and felt it was time he did.

Seth called Darrell before they left to check on the college kids from yesterday. They had arrived and were on their way.

Dressing quickly, Liz and Seth set off for the USF campus. He turned west onto Clark Road, heading for the USF campus on Tamiami Trail.

The Alligator Dance

"I thought about closing the park. Maybe I should have," Liz worried about her decision to keep it open. Maybe she should have pressed her captain, but there were so many other things to deal with.

"No, not the whole park, but I think we should have closed that section to visitors," Seth replied. "I didn't think fast enough."

They were both worried about the college kids hiking out to Gator Hollow that morning. Anything could happen. The boys could run across a momma alligator protecting her nest, or maybe the poachers had returned.

"You can't second guess yourself now. I'm pretty sure the poachers won't be coming back for a while. You did say it was unusual for that kind of activity in a state park. I know I've not heard of it before."

"Right, the parks are pretty safe," Seth said. "I'll talk to Darrell, and maybe we can get Stan to patrol around there more often—especially in the mornings. Maybe that's all it will take to push the poachers to move somewhere else."

"That's good for your park, and I know you will do your best to help, but what about the places that have no protection in a park?" Liz said heatedly, tossing her head back and clenching her fists. "I have a responsibility to find these guys and stop the illegal trade in eggs." Liz hated to see people abuse wildlife, and break the laws set down to protect them. Seth seemed to feel the same way and that was

The Alligator Dance

one of the reasons she admired him. Liz was developing feelings for him. What they were leading to, she wasn't sure.

"Don't worry, you'll get them, and I want to help any way I can." Seth gave her hand a squeeze, holding on to it a bit longer than necessary. He wanted to hold more than her hand.

The Alligator Dance

Chapter Twenty-four

After wending their way through the traffic, they arrived at the USF Admissions Office. Liz showed the receptionist her credentials. "I'm Officer Liz Corday, and this is Ranger Grayson. We are investigating the death of Landon March. We understand that he was a student here and are hoping to locate some of his friends to help us out with some information."

"Why are the FWC and a park ranger investigating a student's death?" asked the receptionist. The nameplate on the desk read: Wilma Jenkins. "Isn't that a police matter?" She shoved her glasses back up her nose and looked through files on her computer. Dying to ask more questions, Liz hesitated—as some students were milling around with big ears and cell phones to spread gossip with the speed of light.

Not wanting to get into the gruesome details in front of the crowded office, she chose her words carefully.

The Alligator Dance

"Landon was found dead in the Manasota State Park. We want to find out how he happened to be there and thought his friends might be able to provide some answers."

Seth was pacing the room and reading notices on the bulletin board. He turned to the receptionist and asked, "Are there notice boards like this all over campus?"

"Yes," Wilma answered, adjusting her reading glasses on her nose and looking over the top at Seth. "The students post all kinds of things. They are supposed to be dated and taken down after a month. There is also a website where they can list stuff for sale, apartments for rent, part-time jobs, rooms to share—you know, that kind of thing. Same deal. Take the ad down when the item is sold or after one month. We want to give everyone a chance. All the ads are supposed to go through this office. I have a student aide who helps out in the office sometimes. She is supposed to check over the posting on the website and keep up with the notice boards."

Liz wondered if that's how the poachers recruited Landon. "Could you give us that web address? It would help a lot if we could have a look at the site. Can you also tell us who his student advisor was?" Liz asked. "I'd still like to know more about Landon and his friends."

"I don't know how much the advisor can tell you. There is the student's privacy to consider," Wilma said, handing Liz a note with the website address.

The Alligator Dance

"Well, I'd still like to talk with him," Liz waited, looking the receptionist in the eye. Her law enforcement attitude spoke volumes without a word spoken. The receptionist clicked a few more keys and wrote the name Dean Forrest McKay on another note.

"His office is down the hall, the last door on the left," Wilma said. "I'll let him know you are coming." She knew that Dean McKay would not be pleased. He did not like visitors or students just showing up without an appointment.

Wilma always thought of the dean as a stuffed shirt with old-fashioned ideas. He ran his department like a dictatorship, and no one was allowed to break his archaic rules.

Liz took the note, looked at the name, and tucked it in her shirt pocket behind her badge. "Thank you," Liz and Seth both said as they left the office.

"I can see the wheels turning," Liz said, giving Seth a shoulder bump as they walked down the hall.

"You're thinking the same thing I am. Landon got hired by someone who posted a job on that website or the notice board," Seth said. His nerves were on edge, and he couldn't put his finger on why.

"Right, and how many other young college kids are replying to that same job notice?" Liz answered him.

They stopped in front of a door with a brass nameplate of Landon's student advisor, Dean Forrest

The Alligator Dance

McKay. Seth rapped on the door and waited. They could hear papers rustling inside. Seth knocked louder. The documents stopped shuffling, and a voice shouted, "Go away. I am not taking any appointments this morning."

Liz shouted back, "Dean McKay, this is FWC Officer Liz Corday. I need to speak to you about one of your students. It's a state investigation."

"This better be important. I'm a busy man," McKay shouted, wrenching open the door. He stood there, startled. "You're not the cops. What the hell do you want here? Didn't the receptionist tell you I do not like to be interrupted? This is not acceptable."

"I'm still a law enforcement officer, Dean," Liz said, holding up her badge. "I'm Officer Liz Corday. I'm investigating the death of Landon March. Ranger Seth Grayson is in charge of the state park where Landon's body was found."

"Of all places? And you think I should have some information about that? I'm sorry for the poor boy and his family, but I know nothing of the circumstances or how he came to be in the park." The dean was standing behind his desk, shuffling his papers, not looking at either Liz or Seth. He seemed to be trying too hard to look busy.

Seth tipped his hat but did not offer the man his hand. He quickly took in the certificates and diplomas hanging on the wall. The man apparently wanted everyone to know how educated he was. McKay's attitude told Seth that the dean thought he was better than his visitors, but Seth also read deception and fear in his eyes. Dean McKay was hiding something.

"Wilma told me the news about Landon, but she did not know the circumstances. She called to say you were here and coming to see me. I do not appreciate interruptions to my day," the dean said, taking a seat behind his large antique desk. He didn't offer seats to Liz or Seth, but they sat in two chairs facing the dean anyway.

"We are not releasing that information until we are further along with the investigation," Liz told him. Her eyes barreled into his. The dean looked away, continuing to shuffle papers. Seth admired how Liz took charge of the interview.

"Then how can I help you?" Dean McKay asked. He didn't like answering questions about students alive or dead. "You know there are privacy issues to be considered."

"Yes, we already got that from the receptionist in Admissions," Liz answered. She could feel him putting up walls. "I assure you, sir, I have full police powers anywhere in the state of Florida--including this campus, this office."

She continued, "We are not trying to invade his privacy. He's dead. How about his friends? Let's start there. Can you tell us who he hung around with? We need to talk to them. They might be able to tell us how he ended up dead

The Alligator Dance

in Manasota State Park. His friends might be able to tell us if he had plans to visit the park or meet someone there."

The dean stalled. "What about his parents? Didn't they know?"

Seth was getting antsy. He stood up to read the diplomas on the wall. His back to the dean, the ranger said, "The police in Lakeland contacted them. Landon told his parents he had found a summer job in Sarasota and would see them when he could," Seth said, pacing the room. "Do you know anything about this summer job he had?"

"No, I have no idea," McKay said loudly. Seth could see that the dean was nervous about the direction of the questions, but why? The dean was evasive and rude. He rearranged three stacks of papers. "I know a couple of the students he hung around with. Ask them."

They had hit a nerve, and the dean was trying to get rid of them. Liz waited for McKay to write down the names of Landon's friends and print his class schedule.

"You will find them if you follow Landon's schedule. They usually hang around in front of the Marshall Student Center."

"Thank you, Dean McKay," Liz said, putting the note with the others she had in her breast pocket. She walked out the door Seth held open for her. With the door closed, Liz bent down and pretended to tie her shoe.

"What are you doing?" Seth asked.

The Alligator Dance

Liz put a finger to her lips. She pressed her ear to the door and listened. Standing up, Liz hurried with Seth down the hall and out of the building.

The Alligator Dance

Chapter Twenty-five

"What do you think about the dean?" Liz asked as they were walking back to the parking lot.

"He was more than nervous with our questions. I want to get back to the park."

"I heard him call someone as soon as we left. He was nervous and shouting at someone. I'd love to know who he called. But I'll never get a subpoena for his phone records with what we have so far."

Seth was convinced the dean knew more about Landon and how he came to be at the park than he was letting on. He would have to talk to Liz about it later. Maybe she could talk her captain into getting those phone records somehow.

"What about talking to Landon's buddies? They might know where Landon found that job," Liz asked as they walked back to Seth's truck.

The Alligator Dance

"I don't think they're going anywhere."

"I'm going to pull up that web address the receptionist gave us and see what I can find there, too. You never know," Liz said, taking the paper out of her pocket and looking at the address. "We've got leads but nothing that gets us very far. We'll just have to keep digging."

"We can come back on my next day off. I'll drop you at my house, and you can pick up your truck if you want or come with me to the park first. I want to talk to Darrell and see if those kids made it out of the preservation area safely."

"Right, I'll go with you to the park and pick up my truck after if that's OK."

Seth was secretly pleased Liz wanted to go to the park first. He was hoping he could talk her into staying over another night—or longer. He had never had thoughts like this before about any woman. It scared him. He didn't know what he was going to do about them.

The Alligator Dance

Chapter Twenty-six

Seth stopped his truck in front of the ranger station. Darrell was sitting at a picnic bench in the shade of the ancient oak tree with Jeff, Joe, and Mike.

Salty sweat stains marked the young men's Columbia University tee shirts as they gulped down bottles of cool water after their hike.

Darrell waved Seth and Liz over. "You guys have to hear what happened out at Gator Hollow to these guys this morning."

"Oh, man, when we got there, it was amazing to see all those alligators," Joe said in his strong Bronx accent.

"Never mind the gators," Jeff spoke up. "What about that creepy guy who tried to run us off?"

"What creepy guy?" Seth and Liz said together.

They looked at each other, instantly knowing it must have something to do with the poaching.

95

The Alligator Dance

"Right, I checked, and there were no other visitors on the list for today," Darrell said. The ranger got up from the picnic bench. "I even double-checked to see if Stan had let someone in and not booked them in properly."

"OK, so tell me about this creepy guy that was trying to run you off," Seth said. He was getting impatient and had a bad feeling about what had happened out there. The college kids were excited—all of them trying to talk at once. Seth was confused and tried to speed things along. Helping Liz find a seat on the bench, he sat down beside her. Under the tree, it was a few degrees cooler, but the breeze from earlier had dropped, and the humidity climbed. It had to be close to a hundred percent.

"Can you get us some water, Darrell? We all need some," Seth said.

When Darrell left, Seth tried to get some sort of order and continued, "Tell me, one at a time," he said to the young men.

"Mike was the first to see them," Jeff said.

"Yeah, there were five of them who looked like workers: laborers or lawn guys. Tree workers, you know, Hispanic, maybe. They were dressed in dirty jeans and heavy boots with old sun hats on. The men all carried these plastic trays. Like big egg cartons, you know what I mean?"

"Yeah, the trays were about this big." Mike spread his hands to show a tray about two feet long.

96

The Alligator Dance

"Yeah, this other guy with a beard and dark glasses, he seemed to be in charge. They were poking around the underbrush a few feet from the edge of the river. I tried to be friendly and said hi," said Joe.

Jeff broke in, "This old official-looking one, he had a kind of Hispanic accent, came over to us and asked us what we were doing there," Jeff said. "It seemed odd that they were questioning us—like we were trespassing or something."

"We told them we had permission from the park ranger to be there. That upset the older man. He got nervous," Joe said.

"Yeah, he started looking around. You know, like he was worried about being seen or something. It was really odd," Mike added.

"The rest of the men had moved along, but this man stood in our way, blocking us. He said that he was a biology professor from a local college, never did give the name of the college. Did he?" Mike asked, turning to Jeff.

"No, he didn't," Jeff agreed. "He said his name was Dr. Melendez, and they were researching alligators and their nesting habits."

"It was Joe who noticed that the five men were coming back with these trays. When they passed us, Joe said he saw eggs in them," Mike said. "A couple dozen were in each—covered with pine straw and grass. Grayish. Maybe

The Alligator Dance

bigger than most chicken or duck eggs. Two to three inches around. They had to be alligator eggs."

"We didn't think much about it, stayed to take a few pictures, and then headed back. The men seemed to have disappeared. We didn't see them on the trail again, either. It was kinda spooky."

"Could you ID the man who said he was a doctor?" Liz asked.

"Yeah, I think so." The college kids all agreed.

"They vanished into thin air—like we said. It was odd. We told the ranger here, and Ranger Harris told us about some guys who steal gator eggs in the park. We couldn't believe it," Joe said.

"I'll have photos faxed to the Tampa office. Can you go have a look at them?" Liz said.

"Sure, if we can do it before we fly home to college," Jeff said.

"Give me some contact numbers, and I'll see what I can do," Liz told them. She stood up and was already on the phone to her headquarters in Tallahassee, requesting to send the photos to Tampa.

Seth stood and thanked the young men. As they were tossing their packs into their car, Liz approached. "I talked to my commander, and he's getting things moving on his end. He also said that if this pans out and we arrest someone for stealing gator eggs, you could be in for a reward."

The Alligator Dance

The mention of a reward got Joe's attention. "Really, how much? Sorry, we didn't report it for that, but I'm just a poor college kid on a scholarship. Every little bit helps. Tuition, beer, clothes, you know. Essentials," Joe said with a laugh.

Liz reached out and touched Joe on the shoulder. "I understand. Believe it or not, I was a poor college student, too, at one time."

"Me too," Seth echoed as he walked around the car, shaking hands with each. "We appreciated you reporting what you saw. We need more folks to step up and do the right thing."

Liz stood beside Seth, thanking the young men. She took the time for a little alligator education.

"I do appreciate your help with this. Poaching in the state park is something new. Male alligators are pretty promiscuous and will mate with several females. Their mating is called the 'alligator dance.' They roll around and round in the water, like a dance." Liz smiled. "The females are good mothers and watch over the nests and hatchlings. The babies grow slowly, and it takes years for them to mature to be able to breed. We do need everyone to respect the wildlife here. Thanks again, guys," Liz said.

Liz and Seth stood in the dust as their convertible pulled out of the park—music blasting, soda cans popping,

The Alligator Dance

stories rolling. Walking back to the ranger's office, Liz said, "This may be the break we have been waiting for.

The Alligator Dance

Chapter Twenty-seven

It was a weekday and pretty slow. Darrell was picking up water bottles and emptying the trash can beside the picnic bench. "Why can't they hit the can? It's right there," he grumbled.

"Hey, you guys care to stop in for a cup of stale coffee or water before you take off?" Darrell shouted, dragging the trash can liner out and tying up the top. It was his job before leaving for the night.

"Sorry, I need to get back to my office and write up a report," Liz said. "I have a date tonight, so I better get a move on."

A date? Seth was disappointed she wouldn't be staying another night at his place. He should have known she had a boyfriend. She was too good-looking and too smart not to have someone. It caught him by surprise that he might be jealous of her boyfriend. Did his feelings for Liz run that

The Alligator Dance

deep? It surprised him that they might after such a short time. Could feelings heat up that quickly?

"Give me a ride to pick up my truck, and I'll be on my way," she said, smiling. She had no idea of her effect on him. She took off her olive green FWC baseball cap and shook out her hair. Seth watched it cascade around her face; streaks of gold flashed in the late afternoon sun.

Darrell watched Liz get into Seth's truck, "Oh, you poor guy. You have no idea what's happening to you, do you?" The ranger chuckled to himself, tossing the trash bag into his vehicle to drop off on his way home. Darrell couldn't wait to tell his girlfriend, Marcia, the development between Liz and Seth. She would be delighted.

The Alligator Dance

Chapter Twenty-eight

Pulling up to his house, Seth asked Liz, "Do you want a cold drink or a coffee before you go?"

"Thanks, but no, I want to beat the traffic to Tampa," Liz glanced at her watch. It was coming up to rush hour.

Nokosi ambled off the porch as Seth parked. Getting out, he gave the dog a good scratch along his back. Liz laughed at the look of pure ecstasy in the dog's eyes.

"Come on, old thing," Seth said, leading the way into the house. His steps slow, knowing Liz was leaving and he would be alone again. Seth liked having Liz there. He felt comfortable with her, needed her. But she already had someone, and he would not interfere.

Seth filled the dog's bowl with clean water and stood, gripping the kitchen counter and looking out the window.

"I'll be right back." Liz walked back through the house to the spare bedroom to collect her things.

The Alligator Dance

Seth stood watching a couple of squirrels chase each other up the oak tree dripping with Spanish moss to their nest high in the branches. *If only life was as simple as that.*

Liz startled him by dropping her duffel bag. "I've got all my stuff, I think. If you find anything, give me a call."

Seth picked up her bag. He held the kitchen door for her and walked Liz out to her truck. Handing her the duffel as she opened the door, he said, "Keep me posted on what you find out on your end. I'll make it over to the college and check out Landon's friends."

Liz stole a look at Seth and wondered what it would be like to kiss him as she buckled herself in and started the engine "Right, with everything else, I forgot about them. Landon's friends might still be worth checking out. They might know how Landon found out about the job with the poachers. But I don't think he knew right away that he was going to be working for poachers. Do you?" Liz asked.

"No, maybe not, but I'm going to find out who hired him," Seth said.

"We're after the same person from different angles," Liz said. She reached down to say Goodbye to Nokosi. "I've got to go. I'll be in touch soon."

Before she got in, Liz stepped and gave Seth an awkward hug. A handshake was not going to do it, and a kiss didn't seem appropriate...yet.

The Alligator Dance

Straighten up. You have a date tonight, and you are not a two-timing hussy.

Seth and Nokosi watched as Liz turned toward Tampa. Walking back to the house, he talked to Nokosi.

"I should have guessed she would have a date now and then with someone, right? I can't expect her to sit around, waiting for me. Jesus, Nokosi, I should have done something, anything. Shit, I don't want her dating anyone. But what the hell am I going to do about it?" He sat on the porch for a bit to watch the squirrels torment Nokosi before giving in to hunger.

Walking into the kitchen, he asked, "Well, Nokosi, it's just you and me again. How 'bout sharing a nice barbecue chicken with me tonight? Baked potato or rice with that?"

The Alligator Dance

Chapter Twenty-nine

The phone rang as he walked into the kitchen. "Hi, Mom," Seth said. "What's up?"

"We're going to practice a dance for the festival next month. Can you come? You remember the Alligator Dance?" his mom asked. "Helen Treadway will be there. Remember how you played together as children? She has a new job at the casino. She's still not married yet, you know."

"I can tell when you are matchmaking, Mom," Seth smiled. He loved his mom, but she was always trying to match him up. His mother wanted him to settle down with a sweet Seminole girl and raise a bunch of grandkids for her to spoil. Thankfully, his dad stayed out of his love life and just wanted him to be happy.

The Alligator Dance

"Maybe a little," Rowena said. "You dated in high school until you both went off to college. Maybe still something there? Maybe?"

"It's been a while since I've seen that dance," Seth said. "We've something going on here. I'll try to make it. Is Dad dancing this time?" Seth's dad, Andres, loved his tribal culture and knew most of the old dances.

"I couldn't stop him if I tried," Rowena laughed. "A couple of your cousins are dancing too. You haven't seen them in ages, and they came from Big Cypress. Getting some of the family together would be fun. Please try, my heart."

"I'll try, Mom," Seth told her. He wanted to see his family but did not enjoy his mother's matchmaking. It always made him feel awkward, and he hated turning away the women his mother threw at him.

"Is it OK if I bring a friend with me?" Seth thought it was a way of seeing Liz away from work and getting to know her better, and she could see the Indian side of him and his culture. It would depend on how attached she was to that date she was on.

"A girlfriend, I hope."

"Mom, she's someone who I'm working with and happens to be a friend. Don't go reading more into it than there is."

The Alligator Dance

Chapter Thirty

He took the chicken pieces out of the fridge, dusted them with seasoning, and went out to start the gas grill. Nokosi barked and ran to the front door. Balancing the chicken plate above the dog's nose, he opened the kitchen door. Liz had returned.

"Back for chicken? I thought you had a date?"

"I did," she nervously kicked the tire of her FWC truck. "I canceled it. I drove almost all the way home. Suddenly, I didn't want to be there. I wanted to be here, with you and Nokosi."

Blushing, she looked at the confusion on Seth's face, "I should go." Liz was embarrassed by her boldness. Liz had never been the pushy type and could not imagine what had made her come back to Seth. He might not want her there. Worse yet, Seth might already have someone he was serious about. Maybe he was cooking for someone else tonight. God, she hoped not.

"Ah… no," Seth stammered. "Please stay. Nokosi and I want you to stay." He looked at the plate in his hands and shook his head. "I hope you like barbecue chicken."

"Sure, need any help?"

"How are you at opening a wine bottle?"

"I can manage that." She was happy that she had made the right decision to cancel her date.

The Alligator Dance

Chapter Thirty-one

Liz and Seth sat at the kitchen table, finishing off the wine. She was again surprised that Seth knew how to pick a good wine to go with the chicken. A delicious Spanish Rioja. "How do you know about wines?" Liz asked.

Seth sat back in his chair and looked at the wine swirling in his glass. "I dated this girl Britney, from California for a bit in college. Her father owned a winery in the Sonoma Valley."

"I always wanted to take a trip there," Liz broke in.

"I never did understand why she was going to a college on the other side of the country until Britney broke down one night and told me that her father had married again after divorcing her mother." Seth sipped long and stifled a chuckle.

"Oh, oh, that usually means trouble."

The Alligator Dance

"The new stepmother was two years younger than her. Britney was hoping he would come to his senses and get rid of the *money-hungry bimbo*. Her words, not mine," he replied.

"Anyway, she taught me about wine, and now I enjoy a good wine once in a while."

"Well, I'm very grateful you do," Liz said, raising her glass to salute him.

"I almost forgot," she continued. "The Tampa office called to tell me they may have a lead. Mike and his friends have an appointment to go in tomorrow and see if they can ID the man they saw in the park."

"That could be hard, seeing as the suspect had on dark glasses and a beard."

"What about going back to see Landon's friends at USF?" Liz asked. She took some of the dishes to the sink. Seth got out food for Nokosi, who had been waiting patiently under the table for anything that might fall his way. He cut up the leftover chicken, added it to the dog's dish.

"We need to do that, too. What's your day look like tomorrow?" Seth said. Liz was at the sink washing up.

Seth watched Liz, hands in the soapy water. He wondered again what it would be like to have someone permanent in his life. Liz stole a look and caught him watching her and smiled.

The Alligator Dance

Seth was looking at his feet when he asked her, "I don't suppose you would like to take a trip out to the reservation this weekend? My mom and dad are practicing the Alligator Dance for a Seminole festival. They asked me to come," Seth said, hopefully. "It's one of the old tribal dances we still perform at the festivals." He wanted to see how things might go with Liz. It was encouraging that she had canceled her date to come back. Taking Liz to the dance might also stop his mother from matchmaking.

Liz turned off the water tap and dried her hands on a towel before answering.

She looked thoughtful and reflective. "Why not? It might be fun. That is, if we don't find any more body parts and if we go to the college and talk to Landon's friends."

"Yeah, a big *if*. Are you staying again tonight?" Seth asked.

"I am *if* you're asking."

The distant rumble of thunder broke the silence. A flash of lightning brightened the room. Liz jumped. "Besides, I'm afraid of thunder and lightning. I don't want to drive home in a storm."

"Just a summer storm. Here and gone before you know it. You're a Florida girl, right?"

"I am, but I've always been afraid of the storms. The sky gets so black and forbidding," Liz stopped to smile and giggle. "When I was six, I used to hide in the closet. My dad would coax me out and tell me I was silly."

"Growing up on the rez, my parents and I would sit on the porch and watch the storm rolling in. We would count the seconds between the lightning strikes and the thunder. I was told that for each second, the storm was that many miles away."

"It's something I can't seem to get over. I'm the same with loud noises like the Fourth of July fireworks. I love the colors in the sky but hate the sound of them going off. I know it's silly."

"It's not silly at all. We all have something that scares the hell out of us."

"What's yours?" Liz asked.

"My mom playing matchmaker. I never know who she's going to try to fix me up with next," Seth laughed. "Anyway, my father told me many of the myths from our culture. They helped me to find a kind of connection to the rhythm of the storms and their purpose in nurturing the land. Along with the way the animals and nature interact."

"Can we sit for a while, and you can tell me some of those myths?" Liz smiled and relaxed. She felt so comfortable here with Seth just talking. Just the sound of his voice soothed her.

"Sure, we have a couple of glasses of wine to finish off."

The Alligator Dance

"Glad I'm not driving tonight." Liz let Seth refill her glass.

"After that, we need to plan on going to the college tomorrow. I'll call Darrell and have him cover for me. I'll bribe him by offering to take one of the overnight campouts later in the Fall." Seth laughed, taking two glasses and the half-empty bottle, and moving to the couch.

He patted the seat next to him. Liz tilted her head, questioning his motives.

Another flash of lightning and a rumble that shook the house had her jumping to sit beside him. She buried her face in his chest. He smelled musky and slightly of the soap from the shower. Seth put his arms around her and stroked her soft sandy hair. She tipped her face up to his. Seth kissed her gently and reveled in the sweet taste of her lips. The subtle flavor of the wine lingered there.

Liz reached up and tenderly ran her thumb over the parallel scars on his cheek. "Tell me about these."

"Really?" Seth paused. "OK. When I was about nine or ten, I was playing catch with some friends on the rez. I missed the ball, and it rolled into the high brush and palmettos bordering the field. When I leaned down to pick it up, a rattler struck me."

"Oh, Seth." Liz stroked the scar.

"My mom saw me holding my face. Blood was dripping through my fingers and down my cheek. She took

114

The Alligator Dance

me to an old healer, Ann Billie. It was horrible. She cut the bite marks to let the venom out, but it was a dry bite, thank goodness. Ann packed the cuts with some herbs, dressed it, and sent me home. I could have been in big trouble if that snake had given me a fatal bite. But it left me with the scars—and deep respect for snakes."

"They did that?"

"It's the part of our culture, the old ways." Seth shook his head and smiled. "We are being dragged kicking and screaming into the twenty-first century, but it's hard for the older generation."

"I can see what you mean."

Seth was comfortable with Liz beside him. Maybe too comfortable. That tender kiss had him wanting more. He still didn't know exactly what he wanted or even if he wanted a relationship.

More importantly, how did she feel about him? Was he just a coworker? A friend, a possible lover, more? He had no answer. But he sure hoped he found one soon.

The Alligator Dance

Chapter Thirty-two

Liz woke and followed the aroma of coffee brewing. She padded out of the guest room to see Seth scrambling eggs. "Hey there, sleepyhead," Seth called. "There's fresh coffee in the pot and bread in the toaster. Can you pop it down for me?"

She pressed the bread down and went to fill her cup. "Thanks for holding me last night and for being a gentleman and not taking advantage," she managed to stammer. Seth managed to get up before her. Some day she hoped to surprise him with a cooked breakfast.

"Believe me, I thought about it," Seth winked as he leaned into the counter. "I like you, Liz. A lot. More than anyone else, in a very long time. But I don't collect conquests like scalps on a pole. Knowing you are sleeping in the next room is comforting, strange, and driving me crazy all at the same time." Seth said all this with his back to her, afraid he would lose the courage to admit his feelings if he looked in her eyes.

"Seth," Liz left her chair to put her hands on his shoulders to turn him to face her. "Don't be afraid of me. I'm not sure of my feelings either, and I'm happy you are willing to let me, us, figure out how we feel about each other."

"You're right about that," he managed. He dipped his head to touch his head to hers and pushed her gently away. They stood facing eachother at arm's length.

"Circumstances have thrown us together, and I have a duty to solve Landon's death and his involvement with the poachers before we can see if there is more for us," Liz said. Seth raised her chin so he could look at her face. He wiped a tear from the corner of her eye.

"You are an amazing woman, Officer Corday. I hope there is an *us*," Seth said, rubbing his thumb over her lips. Just as he lowered his head to kiss her, Nokosi scratched at the door. The dog had finished his early morning hunt for squirrels, and his timely arrival broke the tension. They rested their foreheads together again and laughed, thankful for the interruption.

They finished breakfast, cleared up the kitchen, left water out for Nokosi, and headed out for USF and Landon's friends.

The Alligator Dance

Chapter Thirty-three

Seth and Liz arrived at the USF campus in Sarasota to look for Landon's friends. Liz had their class schedules and asked passing students the way to the Marshall Student Center. It was as good a place as any to start. One young lady they stopped knew Landon's friends. "Yeah, I know Luke Jenkins. Barry Andrews, too. The student center is up there on the right. They usually hang around the center. What do you want them for? They run over a squirrel or something?" she laughed, noticing Liz was FWC.

"Nothing like that," Liz replied.

"I guess we do stand out a bit," Seth said.

Finding the center, they walked down the hall and asked about Jenkins and Andrews. A couple of students were sitting at a table eating lunch with their books scattered around them.

The Alligator Dance

"Yeah, those two are usually gaming in the lounge," a young Asian girl told them. "Follow the noise, and you'll find them wasting their time, as usual." She spoke, not looking at Seth or Liz. She bit her apple and continued to turn the pages of her textbook.

Seth followed the sound of the shouting and noise of a video game. "Over this way," Seth said, motioning to Liz.

They stood in the doorway and watched Luke and Barry noisily playing a futuristic war game on a big screen. There was a lot of gunplay and a loud blast coming from the screen. Seth wondered about the hearing loss these two idiots might be suffering, never mind the brain cells they were destroying.

Seth and Liz both called to the young men. Liz ran out of patience and stood in front of the fifty-inch screen. Barry yelled and motioned at her to get out of the way, "Hey, we're playing a game here."

"Yeah, I'm winning," Luke shouted, jumping up and trying to look around Liz. "I'm about to attack his outpost."

Seth pulled the TV's electric plug. Luke and Barry went ballistic. "Why'd you do that, man?" Luke said. He took off his ball cap and threw it at Seth. Luke ran his hands through his dark greasy hair.

"We need your attention. We have some questions for you," Liz said.

The Alligator Dance

"And who the hell are you?" Barry said. He came closer than a foot to face Liz threateningly. Seth stepped between them and caught a whiff of Barry's unwashed body.

Making a face and waving a hand in front of his nose, Seth asked, "Wow, when's the last time you had a shower?"

Barry stopped to think. His face showed deep concentration as he tried to come up with the answer.

"Must be about three days ago," Barry said.

"Yeah, we had a class that day," Luke agreed.

"Do you know Landon March?" Liz asked.

"Yeah, we have a couple classes with him. Haven't seen him in a couple days," Barry told Liz, throwing down the controls in his hands.

"Who are you, and why do you want to know?" Luke asked. He was the least volatile of the two.

"I'm Florida Wildlife Conservation Officer Liz Corday, and this is Ranger Seth Grayson."

"So, what's that got to do with Landon?" Barry asked. His attitude and tone were telling Liz that he knew more than he was letting on.

"We found Landon's body in the Manasota State Park on Monday," Seth said.

"Ah shit," Luke said, sinking down on to the well-used couch. Barry held his head in his hands, shaking back and forth. "How did he die?" Barry asked softly, still with

The Alligator Dance

his head down. The news of their friend death had shocked them.

"We are not positive, but it looks like an alligator attacked him," Seth answered.

"Any idea what he was doing in the park?" Seth said.

Barry and Luke looked at each other, and a wall came down. "No idea," Barry said, looking at Luke. They were hiding something.

Luke looked up at Seth, "Landon told us he had found a part-time job working for this guy. Said he could do the job early and be back in time for class." Barry glared at Luke for giving out the information.

"Look, Landon was an OK guy. He needed some money fast. He said he owed some money to a badass bookie who wanted to be paid or else," Luke volunteered. Barry shrugged and shook his head.

Liz and Seth both knew the boys were hiding something or afraid to tell what they knew.

"You have any idea where he found this job?" Liz asked.

"There's a notice board up by the coffee bar," Luke said. He fingered the game controller nervously, not looking up at either Liz or Seth. Barry slugged him hard on the shoulder. Seth figured they got about all they could from the pair and plugged the TV in before leaving.

The Alligator Dance

They left the kids to their game and walked over to the notice board. It took a couple of minutes of shuffling through all the posters and flyers before they found what they were looking for. "Here it is," Liz said, holding up a notice to expose the one underneath.

Seth read the notice on an index card. "Great pay for a couple of hours work. Early morning before class. Outside, working with animal research professor." Seth handed it to Liz.

"Barry and Luke know more than they wanted to tell us," Liz said.

"I got the same feeling," Seth agreed. "Let's call this Carl Mickelson person and see where it leads. I want to know who put the notices up on the boards and if they are on that USF job website."

The Alligator Dance

Chapter Thirty-four

Back in the truck, Seth started the engine, turning the air conditioning on high. It was like an oven after sitting in the sun for a couple of hours. "Thank God for air conditioning. I don't know how the early settlers stood it." Liz said, wiping the sweat from her face. After a few minutes, they cooled down, and drove back to Seth's place.

On the way, they discussed plans for going to the reservation that evening and decided that Liz would drive back to Tampa to change her clothes, and Seth could pick her up at her condo.

"What do people wear to these things?" Liz didn't want to be overdressed or underdressed.

"Jeans are fine. The practice dances are very casual," Seth told her. He was looking forward to seeing her in something other than her uniform.

The Alligator Dance

Nokosi lumbered off the porch to greet them as they pulled in. "Hi there, boy, did you miss us?" Seth asked. Nokosi shook all over, and Liz laughed at the dog's happy grin.

"I'm going to hit the road for Tampa. I'll text you my address," Liz said, tapping away on her phone. "What time should I be ready?"

"About 6:30. We can grab a bite at the casino before meeting my parents."

"Perfect, I'll be ready," Liz stood there, not quite sure what to do. She knew what she wanted to do. Taking Seth's hand in hers and looking into his deep gray-green eyes, he read the silent message and kissed her. And oh, it felt so good and so right. He didn't want the kiss to end. Reluctantly pulling away, Liz got into her truck, waved at Seth and Nokosi, and backed out, heading for her place.

"What are we getting ourselves into, my friend?" Seth said to the dog. Getting dressed for a date was something he had not done in a long time. Standing in the shower, his head pressed against the tiles, the hot water cascading over his head, he wondered if his parents would like Liz? After all, she was not Seminole. *Was he getting ahead of himself?* Could meeting Liz put a stop to his mother's matchmaking or ramp her up to *when are you getting married* mode? He didn't want to give his mother false ideas. What if they didn't approve since she was not

The Alligator Dance

Seminole? Did he want them to approve of her as a future wife? *Whoa, where did that come from?*

He buttoned his shirt and looked in the mirror. His shirt was in tones of blue with bright yellow, orange, and touches of red in the Seminole patchwork style, which made his eyes sparkle. "Hmmm, not bad, Nokosi. You think she'll like it?"

Brushing a few dog hairs off his black jeans, he picked up his truck keys and opened the door.

"Take care of the place while I'm gone, OK?" Nokosi looked up at him and woofed.

His GPS talked him right to Liz's condo building. He was nervous getting out and took a moment to slow his beating heart. "Here goes," he encouraged himself as he walked up the stairs to the second floor and knocked.

It took a moment for Liz to answer. His breath caught when he saw her out of uniform. Her turquoise top showed off her sandy hair and eyes. A silver necklace in a Southwest design was an excellent complement.

Stepping in the door, Seth lifted her chin and gently kissed her lips. The taste of her cherry lip gloss surprised him.

"Come in. Almost ready," Liz said. "I just have to grab my purse and keys."

Seth had to admire the way her white jeans showed off her trim figure and long legs. Much better than the plain

The Alligator Dance

khakis uniform. While Liz hunted for her keys, Seth looked around. He noticed how neat and tidy her condo was with little decorations. He was looking out the large picture window that overlooked a large pond with sabal palms and a couple of picnic benches.

"Right, I'm ready," Liz said, gliding out of her bedroom.

"Great view."

"Yeah, when I'm here to enjoy it. I travel a lot for work. The condo is more a place to keep my clothes, not a home." Liz looked around with a sad expression. Seth wondered if she was just waiting to find the right place to call home.

He opened the door and let her go first. The aroma of her perfume as she passed him was light and flowery and oh, so intoxicating. He inhaled the fragrance and hoped he could keep his hands to himself on the drive to his parents.

The Alligator Dance

Chapter Thirty-five

Turning onto I-275, they drove to the Seminole Hard Rock Casino two exits away. His parents owned a double-wide mobile home in a park across from the glittering hotel. The dance practice would be in the community center there. He found a parking space quickly and dashed around to open her door. "A gentleman again. I could get used to this," Liz exclaimed.

Seth laughed at Liz's wide-eye stare when they entered the casino.

"I've never been here before. Only driven past it," said Liz.

"I've come a couple of times with friends. Gambling is not my thing. It's a waste of money and too noisy for me." He led her into the Café, where they followed the hostess to a back booth.

The Alligator Dance

Liz looked the menu over, "Some good choices here. Everything looks great."

They each ordered white wine, and Seth added an appetizer combo of fried gator, citrus chicken kabobs, and conch fritters.

"Tell me a little about your mom and dad. Did they always live on the reservation here in Hillsborough?"

"My mom grew up on the Big Cypress Reservation on the edge of the Everglades. My dad visited some cousins and met her at a dance there."

"Seems like you have a lot of cousins."

"Well, Mom had five brothers and a sister, and Dad had two brothers," Seth popped a conch fritter in his mouth. "What about you, any brothers or sisters?"

"No, I'm an only and Tampa-born and bred. My parents met in college at USF and stayed in the area. They divorced when I was in high school." Liz picked up the last of the gator bites. "Did you grow up on the Big Cypress Reservation?"

"No, my dad got a job on the rez in Hillsborough. He was on the reservation police force. He retired a couple years ago."

"I heard something about they have their own police force."

The Alligator Dance

"That's right. The rez is like a small city with its own independent government, police, fire department, and even hospital and schools."

"Pretty interesting." Liz finished off her wine and sat back, twirling the stem in her fingers. "I wanted to ask about the card we took off the notice board at the college," Liz said—reaching for a napkin to wipe her fingers.

"I'm going to call the number in the morning," Seth said. "It said to contact Carl Mickelson. I want to find out what part he plays in all this. I heard an alligator farm opened up around Myakka somewhere. I'm willing to bet it's got something to do with all this."

"There is a lot to gator farming. First, you have to get a license. Florida has about ninety licensed farms, but only about a small percentage are producing quality hides. That's where the real money is," Liz said. "Some are for the tourists. There's money to be made there, too."

"I have a couple of ideas about how we can find out what this farm in Myakka is up to," Seth said—as the waitress came by.

The Alligator Dance

Chapter Thirty-six

Outside the casino, Seth cautiously took Liz by the hand as they walked to his truck. He was over the moon when she smiled as he opened the door for her. They stood looking at each other, waiting for the other to make the first move. Liz dropped her head shyly, but Seth tipped her chin up to look in her eyes and gently took her lips with his. Before he knew it, the kiss had deepened. She was responding and driving him crazy with need and desire for more. He broke it off and backed up.

"Wow, did we just do that?" Liz asked, getting her breath back.She was finding it hard to give in to all the emotions Seth was stirring within her. Little by little, he was breaking down the barriers she had carefully put up.

"Yeah, we did," Seth said, smiling. "I think we'll have to talk about this at some point."

The Alligator Dance

"Yeah, we will," Liz said, looking away. She slid in and fastened her seatbelt.

The drive across the street was only a couple of blocks but a long one, both lost in thought. Seth wound through the narrow streets of the mobile home park before coming to a stop in front of a well-maintained, attractive newer home. A distinctively-dressed older woman stepped out to greet them. She wore the colorful traditional dress of the Seminole women: a loose blouse over a full, matching mid-length skirt.

"So glad you could come tonight, Seth. We don't see you as often as we would like," Seth's mother gushed as she gave her son a big hug. "And who do we have here?" she asked, smiling at Liz.

"Mom, this is my friend, Liz Corday. She's an officer with the Florida Fish and Wildlife Conservation Commission. Liz, this is my mother, Rowena Tiger Grayson."

"Oh, don't be so formal. Call me Row. Everyone else does."

"Thank you, Row," Liz said with a happy smile. She instantly liked this friendly woman.

"Come inside and meet Seth's dad. Then we'll go to the community center for the dance practice."

The inside of the mobile home was just as impressive as the outside. Family pictures and decorations proclaimed pride in their Seminole heritage along with modern furniture and harmonizing colors. Old maps of Florida hung on the walls and prints of men and women in Seminole dress. Unique Indian pottery pieces were placed around the room with care.

"You have a lovely place here," Liz said.

"Thank you, Liz. A cold drink before we go?"

"Maybe later, thanks, Row."

"Have a seat for a few minutes," Rowena said. She directed them to a couch with a colorful Seminole blanket.

"I'm so glad Seth brought you tonight. He didn't say he was dating anyone," Rowena pried.

Seth looked at Liz and choked. "Liz and I are working together in the park. Officer Corday is a Florida Fish and Wildlife Conservation Commission Law Enforcement Agent. We had an incident at the park, and I'm helping her with the investigation."

"Oh, I'm sorry. My husband says I'm too nosy for my own good. I'll put a fire under Seth's dad and be right back," Rowena said. She fairly skipped down the hall with thoughts that maybe her son had found someone. She could see the chemistry between them—even if they couldn't.

A few minutes later, an older version of Seth joined them in the living room. Seth's dad was every bit as handsome and dressed in the same style shirt that his son wore. Touches of gray at his temples made his dark eyes stand out.

The older man reached out to greet the couple—smiling sedately.

Seth stepped forward and was wrapped in a crushing hug by his father.

"You need to come around more. Your mother worries."

"I know. I'm sorry, Dad. I'll try to do better."

"Liz, this is my father, Andres Grayson. Dad, this is a friend of mine, Liz Corday. Liz is a Florida Wildlife Conservation Officer. We are working together."

"You should have brought her around sooner, Seth. Maybe it will stop your mother from all the matchmaking shenanigans she gets up to," Andres said, a slight smile crinkling the corners of his eyes.

As Liz blushed, Seth watched her and shook his head at his father. "Can we go to the community center before you embarrass me any more?"

The Alligator Dance

Chapter Thirty-seven

Andres drove them to the center a few streets over. Heads turned when they walked in, and several whispered behind their hands. Seth had not attended any event on the rez in a couple years, and rumors were not a match for seeing him walk in holding hands with a non-Indian girl.

A young woman Seth's age was pushed up to them by her mother. "I see you have brought a friend with you tonight, Seth. You remember my daughter Helen, don't you?" the mother said.

"Yes, I do, Mrs. Treadway," Seth said, touching the brim of his Stetson and tipping his head.

"How are you doing, Helen? It's been a while," he continued. "Liz, Helen and I used to play together as children. Helen, this is my friend, Liz Corday."

The Alligator Dance

"Nice to meet you, Liz, " Helen said timidly—wishing her mother had not made such a fuss in front of Seth and his friend.

Seth wondered if all Seminole mothers played matchmakers for their children.

"Helen is working in the casino now. She's a cashier and has a lot of responsibilities there now," Mrs. Treadway said, grinning and praising her daughter.

"That's great. It's nice to see you again, Helen, Mrs. Treadway. We better go join my parents." Seth tipped his head again and put his hand to Liz's back, showing her to a table by the wall where his parents sat with another couple. Before they got to the table, they were stopped by a stocky, broad-shouldered man glaring at Seth. "My sister's not good enough for you, half-breed? You had to go out and find yourself a white woman to screw with?" The man was so close Seth could smell the beer on his breath.

Seth tried to ignore the man and walk around him. "I'm talking to you, half-breed," the man roared. The community center went silent as heads turned.

Liz took Seth's arm and tried to signal to his parents for help. The last thing she wanted was to be caught in a brawl in front of Seth's parents and friends.

"Look, Tom, I don't want to fight. Your sister and I were over a long time ago. We were kids in school. She's moved on, and so have I," Seth said softly and again tried to walk around the man, broader and heavier than Seth.

Helen Treadway and her mother stepped up behind Tom. "Come on, Tom, there is no need for this. Let's go sit down and enjoy the evening," Helen said, tugging on his arm.

"No, he turned his back on the tribe, his people, my sister." Tom took a drunken swing at Seth and missed, spinning himself into a nearby table of startled couples, spilling drinks, and landing hard on the floor. He looked up, wondering how he got there. His eyes were unable to focus.

"I'm so sorry, Seth, Liz. He's been hitting the drink pretty hard lately. His girlfriend left him a couple months back, and he's having a hard time dealing with it."

"I'm sorry too, Helen," Seth said as he watched a couple of men take Tom out of the building.

"Maybe we should go," Liz said. She was uncomfortable and frightened.

"You know he's always been jealous of you. Seeing you tonight reminded him of what he doesn't have is all," Helen apologized.

"Don't be silly, stay." Helen's mother said, reaching out to touch Seth's arm. "Tom has done this before. He'll do it again. Please enjoy the dance. Your parents are so happy you and your friend are here tonight. They would be so

The Alligator Dance

disappointed if you left. Your cousins are here from Big Cypress. We all miss you."

"If you're sure, thanks," Seth said and hugged the older woman and tipped his hat to Helen. He took Liz by the hand and walked across the floor to join his parents. All eyes in the center were on them as they crossed the floor to his mom and dad. Seth hated being the center of attention. *Could this night get any worse? Old girlfriends, drunken Indians, match-making moms, what was I thinking?*

The Alligator Dance

Chapter Thirty-eight

Andres and another man stood as Liz and Seth approached. "Do you remember George and Mina Tiger Reynolds? Mina used to babysit you when you were little," his dad said to Seth.

Seth smiled and nodded his head, "Hello, Mina, George."

"You grew up nice, Seth," Mina replied.

Seth pulled out a chair for Liz and sat beside her. "I must have been very young. I'm sorry, I don't remember that, but I remember meeting you both over the years. It's been a while." Seth introduced Liz. "This is my friend, Liz Corday."

Luckily the drummers and musicians started up and drowned out the need to keep a conversation going.

The Alligator Dance

Liz and Seth scooted their chairs around so they could see the dancers. Andres and Rowena joined a line of dancers with George and Mina Reynolds and a couple of his cousins. The tone and the rhythm of the music changed. The dancers swirled around the floor in a synchronized stomp dance: two by two, the man on the inside and his partner on the outside.

The vibrations of the drums echoed in everyone's chest. Liz found the rhythm hypnotic. She watched, fascinated as the dancers took off with their left foot and brought the right up to stomp beside it. Unexpectedly, the music changed, and the man turned the woman to the inside of the circle.

Seth smiled as he saw Liz try to imitate the dancers' steps while sitting in her chair. "Want to give it a try?"

"Oh, I don't think so. Afraid I'd mess it up," Liz said.

The music stopped for the dancers and musicians to take a break. Andres and Rowena came back to the table. "What do you think about our dance, Liz?" Rowena asked.

"It's fascinating. Is there a story behind the movements?"

"It's believed two people, maybe lovers, are walking down a trail when an alligator approaches. The man bravely swings the woman out of danger, and they carry on down the trail," Rowena told her. "We are going to dance again. Do you want to try?"

The Alligator Dance

"Andres, dance with Liz," Rowena prodded her husband.

Andres scowled slightly, whispering back at his wife, "You know that is not our way."

"Times are changing. Do this for Seth…and me."

"Please, I don't want to break any rules," Liz said.

"My wife is right. Come."

As the music started up, Andres took Liz by the hand and dragged her off her seat, not giving her a chance to protest. "Come on, Liz, I'll protect you from the alligators," Andres smiled lightly, and Liz could not resist. Seth cocked his brows as they took their place in line.

Rowena held out her hand to her son. "You can't leave me without a partner, can you?"

Seth adjusted his hat and led his mother to join the others.

The line swayed to the music. Liz caught on fast to the changing rhythm and tone of the music and enjoyed the repetitive stomping. She was soon lost in the sheer joy of it. Seth saw the look on her face as she danced with his father.

Seth's mother leaned into him and said, "She may be the one for you," as he turned her away to the inside.

"Mom, you can stop your matchmaking now," Seth whispered in her ear. Rowena took that as a positive sign and smiled, adding a little extra skip to her step.

The Alligator Dance

As the dance ended, they returned to the tables. Liz was breathless and glowing.

Liz and Seth stopped to spend time with his cousins catching up on the gossip for the Big Cypress Rez and the rest of the family.

Noticing the time, Seth returned with Liz to his parents. "It's been fun, but we need to head back. I have work in the morning," Seth said.

"I enjoyed myself. It was so nice to meet you. I have reports to write up and work to catch up on," Liz added. "I'd like to come back again sometime and learn some more dances, Mr. Grayson."

"Please remember, call me Andres. We are friends now."

"Of course, Andres, it is."

"You can come back anytime. Even without my son," Rowena said, "Who never visits his mother." She laughed, pinching Seth's cheek and shaking his head.

"And I may have found a new dance partner," Andres said, touching Liz on the shoulder. Liz, wearing a wide-eyed smile, looked over at Seth, who smiled back. They needed to talk about where this was going. Seth already had a pretty good idea. At least he knew where he wanted it to go. The big question was, did Liz?

"Mom, you and Dad stay awhile. We can walk back to the truck," Seth hugged them, and said goodbye to people

The Alligator Dance

they passed on the way out. Many clapped him on the back or stopped to shake his hand.

Helen came up to them on their way out, "Please don't let my brother keep you away. You are still part of the tribe. We all miss you and want you to come back to visit."

"Thanks, Helen, I appreciate that. I'll see you again soon."

Outside, the Tampa air was still and muggy. "I hope you don't mind walking. I didn't want to pull my folks away from their friends," Seth said.

"I'm fine," Liz told him. "I had a great time, and your parents are wonderful."

"They like you a lot."

"Will you bring me back again?" Liz said, hopefully.

"I better or Mom will kill me," Seth said, laughing. They bumped shoulders as they walked, and Liz took his hand. Seth stopped, looked at Liz, and drew her to him. He stopped under a street light and turned her into his arms, kissing her deeply and passionately.

A man sitting on his mobile home porch across the road yelled at them, "Hey, you two, the hotel is across the street. Get a room."

The Alligator Dance

Chapter Thirty-nine

That set Liz and Seth off giggling as they jogged down the street to his parents' place. Reaching Seth's truck, they jumped in and ramped up the air conditioner. Liz put her face close to the vent to cool down, still smiling and giggling.

Seth sat for a moment, debating about what to do next. His feelings for Liz were growing, but did she feel the same? Reaching across the seat, he took Liz's hand in his and kissed it. *Damn bucket seats,* he cursed.

Liz answered the unasked question. "Your place or mine?"

"Yours, it's closer. And I can't wait," Seth said, backing out of the driveway and heading for Liz's condo.

The Alligator Dance

Chapter Forty

Liz unlocked the door to her condo and walked in, switching on the lights. She turned to place her keys on the table by the door and, in doing so, turned straight into Seth's arms. Liz didn't hesitate to take Seth's lips with hers, her fingers unbuttoning his shirt as she did. They broke away to catch their breath.

"This is what we need to talk about," Seth said. His fingers were on her belt buckle, pulling her close.

Liz looked down at the buttons on Seth's shirt, her fingers shaking as she rebuttoned it. "Oh, God. I can't do this. I like you, Seth, a lot. But I'm not a one-night-stand kind of girl."

The Alligator Dance

"I never thought you were," Seth said, gently and valiantly holding himself together. His body was in agony, screaming for release.

"I thought about this the whole way from the reservation. I thought about what I would do, what I would say." She raised her face to look into his eyes. "I can't believe I'm doing this." Liz turned away, her back to him to hide her tears and shame.

"I wanted you tonight, Seth, and I can tell you want me, too. But I can't." Seth took her by the shoulders and brought her around to face him, watching a tear skim down her cheek. "I feel so stupid. My body says yes, oh God, yes. My heart says yes, but my brain says slow down. If you never want to see me again, I'll understand."

"You don't have to say anything," Seth said. He drew her to him, wrapping his arms around her. Liz relaxed and rested her head on his shoulder. He could feel her heartbeat, the rhythm of her breathing, as one.

Liz sniffed and wiped at her tear. "I'm embarrassed about crying. I'm embarrassed that I didn't go through with it tonight. Seth, I'm so, so sorry."

"Don't feel embarrassed. You're honest, and that's one of the reasons I like you. Yes, I wanted you. I still want you, but I can wait until you're ready." Seth lifted her chin, looking into her eyes, "You're killing me, but I can wait."

The Alligator Dance

Liz stepped away and walked a few paces into the living room. "I was serious with someone awhile back. I thought he was too. Until he broke it off to go with another woman. I thought she was a friend, and it felt like they betrayed me. It took me a couple of years to get over it. I've had a hard time trusting anyone since."

Liz stood with her back to Seth, looking out the big picture window overlooking a retention pond—the lights from the parking lot reflecting on the still water.

Seth followed and turned her to face him again. "You can trust me. I'll never ask you to do anything you are not ready to do."

"I believe that," Liz chewed on her lower lip, afraid and hopeful at the same time.

"Liz, I don't know where this is going between us, but I'd like a chance to find out. Besides, I don't want to disappoint my mother. You are the first person I've brought to meet them. If I know my mother, she's planning the wedding already."

That made Liz laugh, releasing the tension in the room. "I like your parents, too. Wouldn't they want you to marry a Seminole girl?" Liz said, taking a seat on the couch. Seth sat beside her and took her hand, rubbing his calloused thumb over her delicate knuckles.

The Alligator Dance

Chapter Forty-one

"My parents and I fought a lot when I wanted to leave the reservation. My mother understood that young people had to find their own way in the world but still didn't want me to go."

"That's because they love you."

"My father was more stubborn. He wanted me to follow the old ways. But times were changing as I grew up. The Seminoles had the casinos, a police force, their own fire department, and the reservations were becoming small cities with schools and hospitals. My mother saw the changes coming. But still, the culture was important and needed to be preserved. It's like being caught between two worlds."

"Nothing stays the same. Things are changing more each day," Liz agreed.

"Yeah, but my father closed his eyes for many years and refused to see. We fought, and I left first for college and then to work as a park ranger. He has accepted my decisions now but still hopes I will return to the reservation."

"It must have been hard to go against their wishes. Change can be hard to accept," Liz said.

"But we have changed with the times. We no longer leave half-breed children in the Everglades to die," Seth said.

"Did they really do that?" Liz asked, appalled at the thought.

"Yes, they did. Seminole culture has many rules to follow. I've studied our history, listened to the tales from the elders, and not all of it's good."

"I'd like to learn more. It's part of the history of Florida, and it's your history," Liz said.

"Some of the myths and legends go back to the beginning of time. Sorry, I didn't mean to give a lecture," Seth said.

They sat in silence for awhile, holding each other. The only sound was the hum of the air conditioner.

"Look, it's late, and we both have work to do. How about we meet up at the park tomorrow after you get off work? Make some plans. I have some questions about the poachers." Seth stood and pulled Liz up with him.

"Right, I'll bring the supper this time. Maybe even a bone for Nokosi," Liz said. She clutched Seth's hand and did not want to let go. A tear escaped and ran down her cheek.

The Alligator Dance

They stood facing each other, neither wanting to say goodbye and the night to end. Seth broke the silence. "I'm going, Nokosi will be starving, and he needs a run." He opened the door and couldn't resist giving Liz one more light kiss. Liz closed the door, listening to Seth's steps retreating down the hall, wanting to call him back. She leaned against the door and slid to the floor. *What the hell am I doing?*

The Alligator Dance

Chapter Forty-two

"Oh, thank God," a woman cried out, rushing up to Seth as he patrolled the campsites the following morning with Nokosi. "My phone died, and I couldn't call anyone. Our car is back at the ranger station."

She collapsed into Seth's arms. "My husband went for a hike two hours ago. He hasn't come back. I have a bad feeling. Something has happened to him, I'm sure of it," she sobbed.

Seth called Darrell at the station to tell him about the lost camper. "I'll call you back if I don't find him, and we'll organize a search. Can you come to the camp and take a few details?" He hung up and asked the woman, "Which way did he go?" The women pointed down a well-used trail.

"Ranger Harris will be here in a few minutes. I'll look for your husband. He probably just lost track of time.

The Alligator Dance

Try not to worry. It's easy to get turned around. We'll find him in no time."

Seth hit his stride, walking down the narrow hiking trail with Nokosi at his heels, wondering why people insisted on hiking and camping in Florida in the middle of the summer. It could be a hundred in the shade. He hoped the missing husband had water. It could be a case of heatstroke, and that could be deadly.

After half an hour of walking, Nokosi barked and raced ahead. Seth found the man slumped against an oak tree with an empty water bottle in his hand. The man's ankle was hanging at a lousy angle, a bone sticking out the side. Seth felt for a pulse on the ankle. He found nothing. Crouching beside the man, Seth checked again for a pulse in his neck. "He's alive but not doing well," Seth said, looking at Nokosi.

Seth called Darrell. "Get an ambulance to Deer Run trail. We have a badly broken ankle. It's compound and no pulse in the foot." Seth concentrated on saving the man's life. Seth knew from his first aid courses that not having a pulse in the foot was very bad. If circulation was not restored quickly, the victim could lose his foot. It could already be too late.

Seth rubbed the man's chest hard. Finally, the hiker fluttered his eyes and moaned. "Glad you could join us. I'm Ranger Grayson. I have an ambulance coming. Can you take some water for me?"

The Alligator Dance

Seth helped the man to take a few sips of water. "Can you tell me your name?"

"Richard, Richard Johansen," the man croaked out through dry lips.

Another sip of water and Seth asked, "Where are you from, Richard?" Keeping the man conscious was essential to his survival.

"Illinois," he told Seth. The ambulance wailed in the distance. Seth breathed a sigh of relief.

"Hear that, Richard?" Seth said. Richard closed his eyes. "No, Richard, stay with me." Seth tapped him hard on the face. He couldn't let him slip into unconsciousness or, worse, a coma.

"Come on, Richard." Seth slapped him again. "A few more minutes and the medics will be here to take care of you. Your wife is anxious about you. She'll be happy to see you."

The mention of his wife spurred Richard to open his eyes. "Cora, she'll be so mad at me. Pissed."

After what seemed forever, a 4x4 pulled up with two medics. The EMTs went to work, trying to save Richard's life. Darrell, in another 4x4, came to a stop. The victim's wife and his little boy jumped off and ran to him.

As the EMTs and Seth struggled to keep his wife out of the way, Cora yelled over the EMTs, "Richard, I love you."

The Alligator Dance

Stepping back, she whispered to Seth through her tears—clutching her scared little boy to her. "When he gets over this, I'm so gonna kill him for scaring me like this."

It was a bumpy ride on the way back to the trailhead. Once they had the victim loaded in the waiting ambulance, they raced to Sarasota Memorial Hospital—a half-hour away if traffic was light.

Darrell offered to take Seth and Nokosi back to the station with Mrs. Johansen and her son. Seth declined, preferring to walk. Even in the heat, he had some thinking to do and needed the time alone.

The sun was setting when Seth finally arrived at the ranger station. Liz was there, waiting for him, talking to Darrell. As soon as she saw him on the trail, she jumped up and ran to hug him. Seth could see Darrell's eyes widen, smirking knowingly.

"I was worried about you," Liz said, slapping Seth on the arm. "You don't call. You don't send up smoke signals."

"Very funny," Seth said. "No fires on the trail, lady."

"I like her already," Darrell laughed. He could see how things were going even if Liz and Seth couldn't. In the few years he had known Seth, Darrell had never seen him so happy as when he was with Liz.

The Alligator Dance

In the office, Liz sat down in Seth's creaky old desk chair. "Darrell filled me in on the broken ankle. It sounds like a bad one. I hope he pulls through."

"His wife was stressed out about him." Seth stifled a laugh. "She said if he survived, she was going to kill him."

"I would too if you were in that situation." Liz reached out, smiling, taking his hand in hers.

"You mean you'd worry if I was lost in the woods?" Seth said, looking down at their entwined hands.

Liz yanked her hat off and hit Seth with it, hard.

"I guess that's a yes?"

"I'd worry about you because I care what happens to you."

Seth opened his arms, "Aww..." and took Liz in an embrace. He smiled, pleased that she'd worry about him because he cared so much about her, too.

Releasing herself from Seth, Liz asked, "So tell me. How did this poor guy end up in trouble?"

Seth took off his hat and ran his hands through his sweat-drenched hair. "He wasn't wearing hiking boots, only sneakers. It looks like he stepped in a gopher tortoise hole. The next twenty-four hours are critical. I'll call the hospital in the morning. He could lose that foot. I'll have a ton of paperwork for this one."

The Alligator Dance

"Well, I'm starving, and poor Nokosi here is worn out," Liz said. The dog was lying in a corner, his head on his paws, looking up at them.

"Sorry I took so long walking back. I had some thinking to do. Let's go. You mentioned you were cooking tonight?" Seth said. He sure as hell didn't feel like cooking and was looking forward to spending the evening with Liz. Whatever she was dishing up was fine with him.

"Right. I've got things in a cooler. Meet me at your place," Liz said. She stood up and patted Nokosi. "Thanks, Darrell. See you later, gator." She winked.

Seth threw his arm around Liz's shoulder and walked her out. When she opened her truck's door, Nokosi jumped in.

"OK, traitor," Seth laughed. "Guess he wants to ride with you." Seth pecked Liz on the cheek and closed the door. He walked away, shaking his head.

Darrell was chuckling with a big grin. "Oh, this is going to be fun," he said to himself, watching Seth and Liz leave the park.

The Alligator Dance

Chapter Forty-three

Liz and Seth pulled into his yard at the same time. Nokosi flew out and barked at a squirrel chattering away high in a tree.

"Did you bring a whole kitchen in here?" Seth asked as he struggled to carry the cooler up the steps.

"Just a few essentials." Liz was already digging in and taking dishes and containers out.

Seth tried to peek, but she shoved him out of the way. "Take your shower. You stink, ranger," she giggled.

Seth made a face as he sniffed his sweat-stained shirt. "That's bad," and headed to the shower.

Liz cooked a delicious supper. She was setting the table when Seth walked out, bare-chested, still glistening from his shower. Liz took one look and wondered if she would end up in bed with him at some point. The sooner, the better as far as her body response was concerned. Her brain

The Alligator Dance

was another matter—if she could just get them on the same page.

Seth slipped his tee-shirt over his head, "Something smells good, Italian?"

"Good guess. I have lasagna, a salad, and garlic bread," Liz said. "I made the lasagna up while I was working at the condo today. All I had to do was pop it in the oven. We still have about thirty minutes to go. How about you opening one of those bottles of wine?" Liz pointed to a bottle of red on the counter and a couple of glasses, alongside a small antipasto plate.

He took the two glasses into the sitting room along with the antipasto.

"I have an idea. I don't think you'll like it." Seth paused to gulp his wine and pop an olive in his mouth.

"I don't like it already," she answered.

"The way I see it, we need to find out who is in charge of the operation. I need to check out the alligator farm in Myakka," Seth said.

"How do you plan to do that?"

"I'll call that number on the bulletin board. Get hired. That way, I can work on the inside, make myself useful."

"I don't like that idea, but we do need to find out who is pulling the strings. They'll kill you and feed you to the alligators if they figure out who you are," Liz said. She reached over to put her hand on his. "I could check out their

157

permits. If they don't have papers, we could shut them down. We need to run this by Captain Jacobs. You're a civilian."

"We could, but they would just set up somewhere else and start all over again," Seth said—taking her hand.

"You're right. Let's catch these bastards," Liz said, yanking Seth to his feet. "Let's eat first."

The Alligator Dance

Chapter Forty-four

After supper, Seth and Liz cleaned up the dishes, fed Nokosi, and finished off the bottle of wine. Sitting on the couch, neither wanted to say goodnight.

"Liz, I know we agreed to take it slow and see where this goes. So, I think before we let the wine go to our heads, we'd better say goodnight." Seth stood up. He took Liz's hand and helped her up. Looking in her eyes was pure torture for him. He pulled her to him and gently kissed her. He could see into her heart. Her soul. Her desire. And she could read him. He wanted her. Now.

Shaking his head, Seth pushed her away.

"Time for bed." Seth started for his room.

Liz had second thoughts. *Was it time to trust again? Could she trust Seth not to break her heart? She wanted so*

The Alligator Dance

badly to sleep in his arms. Safe and loved. She let a tear escape and run down her cheek, brushing it off.

It took hours to fall asleep, and the eastern sky was beginning to lighten when she finally did.

Liz was not the only one awake. Seth stared at the crack in his ceiling he had meant to fix for weeks. He knew he was falling in love with Liz and wanted her in his life. He wanted to wake up beside her in the morning, every morning. But Liz was not ready, and he would not push her. She had to come to him on her own.

The Alligator Dance

Chapter Forty-five

Seth smelled coffee. Slipping on jeans and a tee-shirt, he followed the aroma as he wiped the sleep from his eyes and padded barefoot out to the kitchen. Standing in the doorway, he followed Liz's movements as she cooked scrambled eggs and bacon.

Turning with a frying pan in her hand, she was startled to see Seth.

"Hey there," she managed. "I have some breakfast ready, and Nokosi has already been out chasing rabbits."

"Thanks, this looks great," Seth said, taking his place at the table. Seeing her hair tousled from sleep had him thinking again of possibilities.

The Alligator Dance

"What are the plans for today? We talked about going to the college to talk to that professor again." Liz began serving.

"Dean McKay was acting very nervous when we talked to him. He made that call as soon as we left. You have to wonder who he called. That notice at the college didn't put itself on the board either. Someone had to put it there. I'll call and see if I can get hired." Seth reached for a full plate.

"Can't talk you out of going undercover, can I? You know it's not in your job description. It should be someone from the FWC Law Enforcement who goes undercover. We have people trained for that. I'll have to call my office and give them a heads up. They might not let you and want to send in a Wildlife Commission officer. You're not a law enforcement officer, after all."

Seth leaned back in his chair, "I've been thinking about that. I may not be law enforcement, but I'm Seminole, and that just might get me hired over a white man," he said, winking at her.

"I'm still going to call headquarters. My commander hates surprises. He has to know what you are planning." Liz left to make the call.

Seth walked out and sat on the step with Nokosi, watching the sky lighten as the sun rose somewhere over the Atlantic. "I have a way of ruffling her feathers. Is she mad at me for wanting to help by going undercover with the poachers, or is she afraid for me because she has feelings for me?" Getting no answer from the dog, he stood. "You're not a lot of help, you know," Seth headed back into the kitchen.

Liz came back from her call as Seth was finishing the dishes and sat at the table, sighing. "My commander is not happy with your idea but understands. He's agreed to your working for the poachers. He even suggested that you might like to apply to the FWC full-time after this is all over." Liz stared down at the phone in her hands. "That is, if you live through this."

Seth wiped his hands on a kitchen towel, casually throwing it over his shoulder. He stood behind Liz and placed his hands on her shoulders, kissing the top of her head. "I have every intention of living through this. Working for the FWC is something I hadn't thought of." Seth threw the dish towel on the counter and faced Liz. "Would I get to wear a bright shiny badge like yours?"

The thought of working for the FWC was intriguing. He had been wondering if being a park ranger was all he wanted to do for the rest of his life. Maybe the FWC was the opportunity he had been waiting for.

Putting those thoughts aside, Seth called the Myakka Alligator Farm about getting hired. He was sitting there holding the phone when she returned to the kitchen. "How'd it go?" she asked.

The Alligator Dance

"I'll meet someone tomorrow afternoon at the alligator farm. I guess they'll check me out and let me know," Seth said.

"How about we go back and try and talk to that Dean McKay again? I want to ask him who puts the notices up and who puts them on the website," he said.

"Good idea," Liz said. "It could be anyone can post on the website, or maybe they have to go through some sort of approval."

The Alligator Dance

Chapter Forty-six

When Liz and Seth arrived at the campus, several vehicles from the Sarasota Police Department and campus security were clogging the road and parking lot in front of the Administration building at USF Sarasota/Manatee with their strobe lights flashing.

"I don't like the looks of this," Liz said.

They walked up to the yellow police tape blocking off a section of the road. Liz approached one of the officers and flashed her badge. "What's going on here?"

"Who wants to know?" A young uniformed officer with no manners asked.

"I'm Office Liz Corday with the Florida Fish and Wildlife Conservation Commission, and my companion is Ranger Seth Grayson." Liz flashed her badge for the young officer.

The Alligator Dance

"Some professor was run down." The officer didn't look up from his notebook. Seth and Liz saw the body, broken and bloody, laying on the road covered with a sheet—blood leaking out, staining the pavement.

"I'm sorry, but we need to know his name. We are on an investigation, and we're hoping to talk to someone here today."

"I'll get someone." The officer walked over to a man in shirt sleeves. A gold badge on his belt flashed in the sun. After a few minutes, a short, stocky Latino man came to talk to Seth and Liz.

"I understand you have some interest here?" he said gruffly. He was the no-nonsense type and showed he didn't like being interrupted while assessing a case.

"As I told your young officer, I'm Officer Liz Corday from the Florida Fish and Wildlife Conservation Commission," Liz said, flashing her badge again. That seemed to soften the man a bit, but not a lot.

"Sorry, lots of curiosity seekers here. I'm in charge of this scene, Detective Ramirez Homicide. The dead man is Dean Forest McKay. He's apparently on staff here."

"That's the man we were coming to see." Liz was stunned.

"It was a hit and run, and he died on impact. Several kids saw it happen." Rameriz nodded to the crowd of onlookers. "All the reports say the same thing. The dean came out of the building, jogging like he was in a hurry to get somewhere."

"Was it just an unfortunate accident?" Liz asked.

"I don't think so. Witnesses said a black SUV was idling by the curb about fifty yards away. As soon as the dean started to cross the lot, the driver accelerated and swerved to hit the victim," said the detective.

Seth tugged on Liz's sleeve, "We better go. Too many people are watching."

Liz understood what he meant. Seth didn't want to be recognized if he would be going undercover, and the killer could very well be watching.

"Thank you, detective," Liz started to walk away.

"Excuse me. Why the interest in Dean McKay?" asked the detective.

"He was helping us with a wildlife issue, that's all," Liz told him. She could fill the detective in later, privately. They walked towards the Administration building to talk with the dean's secretary.

The Alligator Dance

Chapter Forty-seven

Seth got to the door of the dean's office first and knocked on the open door. The receptionist they had seen before, Wilma Conway, was sitting at her desk softly crying into a tissue. She looked up at the sound.

"Sorry, we are not taking any visitors today," she sniffed. "Dean McKay was killed today."

"Yes, we know," Seth said, taking the lead. "We don't want to take up too much of your time."

"Sorry, yes, I remember now," the receptionist said, wiping her eyes.

"Can you tell me who puts the help wanted notices on the bulletin boards? Is there a procedure for getting them on the website?" Seth asked.

Seth's flashing gray-green eyes did the trick, and she opened up to him and stopped crying.

The Alligator Dance

"All the notices are supposed to come through here. I date them for a month in the future. The office assistant is supposed to check the boards once a month, take down the old notices and put up the new ones."

Seth handed her the notice he had taken from the student hall. "Is this one you put up?"

The secretary examined it and handed it back, "No, it's not dated, so I didn't put it up."

"Have you seen any like it on the website or a board?"

The secretary looked thoughtful for a moment and typed on her computer. "Here is one Dean McKay asked me to put on the website." She turned the screen around for Seth and Liz to see.

"I didn't post it. Dean McKay did. He said he was helping a friend," she said.

Seth gave her a big smile, "Thank you so much. You were very helpful." He took Liz by the arm and guided her out the door.

In the hallway heading to the car, Liz said, "Someone killed him to shut him up. That phone call he made tipped the poachers off that we were snooping around. The dean was nervous, and these guys are bad news."

Heading home, Seth said, "We know a couple of answers, but it still leaves us with the big question. Who is running the operation?"

The Alligator Dance

"That's why you're going to risk everything and go undercover?" Liz said, looking out the window. She knew what was at stake and how ruthless poachers could be to protect their business. Some of her fellow FWC officers had been killed in the line of duty. She didn't want Seth to be added to that list.

Seth reached across the seat and took Liz's hand. "I'll be careful. We have a lot to talk about when this is all over."

The Alligator Dance

Chapter Forty-eight

Sitting comfortably in Seth's living room with Nokosi at their feet, Seth asked, "Can you tell me more about how the alligator egg trade works?"

"I'll tell you what I know," Liz said, settling back and getting comfortable. "Some, I'm sure you already know. The Florida alligator was on the US Endangered Species List until 1987. They are doing well now—partly because the state promoted the private alligator farms. There are about ninety licensed farms, but less than twenty that are actively producing hides. The real money is in the hide, not in the meat. Like I said earlier, the big operator is Lousiana. Alligators don't nest well in captivity. The demand and the price for eggs had risen so high that the regulated systems for collecting them in the wild are under a lot of pressure.

The Alligator Dance

Now the prices have dropped dramatically, and more eggs have to be collected to make that profit."

"So, there are legal ways of collecting eggs?"

"Right, there are two ways to get them legally," Liz continued. "The state of Florida issues thirty permits a year. Some have held on to the permits for years. Others hold several permits."

"I guess some pass the permits to their children?"

"Right, the state also determines how many eggs those with permits can collect from public waters each year, and the state says where. They also have to pay the state for each egg collected on top of their cost."

"You said there were two ways?"

"The second way is for a permit holder to gather eggs on private land. They have to pay the landowner a fee for each egg collected and pay for a biologist to check where and how they are collecting."

"I didn't know there was that much to it."

"It's why so many turn to poaching. No red tape to go through and a bigger payout," Liz told him. "My commander told me that the farm in Myakka is reporting hatch rates that are far above the expected level. That can only be achieved by acquiring eggs from outside the farm. Poaching probably."

"Guess I'll find out more tomorrow when I meet with this guy Carl, " Seth said.

The Alligator Dance

After their casual supper, Liz was strangely quiet. Seth knew she was worried about him.

Sitting on the couch, Seth took her hand and, putting it to his lips, gently kissed it. "I'm going to be OK," Seth whispered.

"Hope so. I know what these people can do," she replied. "I want to go to the gator farm after you and pretend I'm doing a regular inspection. What I don't want is for them to pull out and go somewhere else."

Seth helped Liz to her feet, "Get to sleep. We have a busy day tomorrow."

Liz reluctantly padded off to her room while Seth let Nokosi out for his evening run. Seth stood on the porch steps looking up at the full moon. He said a silent prayer that he was not lying to himself or Liz. It could turn out very badly if anything went wrong.

The Alligator Dance

Chapter Forty-nine

It was early in the morning with the sun barely up when Liz hung up from her talk with the FWC captain in Tampa. "Captain Neil Jacobs wants to have a chat before you go to Myakka. He wants to meet with you and brief you on what we need to prosecute these guys. You know, make this case stick."

Seth listened. He was already dressed and in the kitchen. "I'm supposed to meet Carl at 1:00. I won't have time to go to your office and back here before going to the farm." Seth was washing a few dishes. He was absently looking out the window—his thoughts a million miles away. He turned off the tap and, wiping his hands, tried to read Liz.

"He's heading into his office and will be there when you get there," Liz said.

The Alligator Dance

"Coffee's in the pot if you want some," Seth said, refreshing Nokosi's water bowl. "I have a favor to ask. Can you stay here while I'm undercover to take care of Nokosi? I have no idea when I can come back. I'd feel better if you were here with him."

Seth sat in a kitchen chair and called the dog over. "I'm going to try and come home every day, but I don't know what they might have me do. They might only have me collecting eggs for a couple of hours in the morning, or I could be working at the gator farm all day."

Seth had such a sad look in his eyes at the thought of being separated from Nokosi and Liz. Or was he finally realizing the danger ahead?

Liz sat down across from him. "Of course, I'll stay here until this is over."

She stared into her coffee. Liz was afraid if she looked at Seth, she would cry. Captain Jacobs had cautioned her on the possibility that Seth might get into big trouble, even killed. Liz was to inspect the farm after Seth was established. The commander suggested the claim of an inspection by the FWC was valid and that Seth would have more information to give her by then.

"I want you to keep in touch every step of the way. If you can't come home, call me. Please, I'll go crazy worrying about you." Liz stretched her hands across the table, and Seth took them in his.

The Alligator Dance

"No need to panic until you have to. The poachers may not even hire me. I'm not a college kid, and I have to think up some way I found out about the job in the first place."

"What about telling Carl that you have a friend at the college who gave you the number? They knew you needed the money. You need to keep it close to the truth," Liz said.

"I need to go find this place. Carl gave me directions, but it's off the main roads. What are you going to do today?" Seth asked.

"I'll go into the office and write up some reports. I hope you can come up with some names I can research. See if you can get a look at their setup, the incubators for the eggs, and who is their contact in Louisiana."

"Before I forget, the college boys from Columbia went to Tampa to try and ID the man they saw at Gator Hollow. They didn't find a match," Liz said, finishing her coffee.

"It was a long shot anyway," Seth said.

The Alligator Dance

Chapter Fifty

Liz picked up her things, and Seth walked her out. He couldn't let her go like this. He stopped her and drew her to him. "Look, I'll be careful," Seth said, taking a breath and almost choking on his words. "I want you to know I've never felt this way about anyone before. Liz, I think you feel the same way." He stopped talking and looked at his boots. Seth was pretty sure he was falling in love with her.

"Seth," Liz said, putting her hand on his tanned cheek. Her fingers were tracing the scars left by the snake bite years ago. "I do feel like there is something between us. But I'm afraid of going too fast, of trusting too soon. Seth, I thought my parents loved each other, but they divorced. I got to see my father every other Saturday. I loved both my parents, but I was torn between them. I hated that. They didn't do anything wrong, no cheating or anything like that. They just grew apart."

The Alligator Dance

Seth enveloped her in his arms. "I can't promise that won't happen, but I do promise to love you for as long as you will let me. Whoa, I said it. I love you, Liz. I want you in my life. Hell, my mom wants you in my life."

Liz looked Seth in the eyes, laughing lightly, and smiled. "God,help me. I guess I love you too." She rested her head on his chest and could hear his heart beating. Putting her hand over his heart, feeling its rhythm. She raised her face and kissed him, gently at first and then with a passion and desire she didn't know was in her.

"Wow." Breaking free to breathe, she said, "I'd better go, or I'll never leave."

"I'll call you tonight. Promise," Seth told her, watching her buckle her seat belt. Nokosi stood by his side as Liz drove away.

Seth knelt down and took the big dog's head in his hands, looking him in the eyes. "I'd better go too, Nokosi, before the traffic gets terrible. Liz will be back tonight. Hopefully, me, too. You be good. Don't let the squirrels steal the house." Seth laughed at the knowing look in the dog's eyes.

The Alligator Dance

Chapter Fifty-one

Seth made a call to the Manasota State Park. "Hi, Darrell," Seth said when the young ranger answered. "I'm taking a week of personal time. Stan will be happy to take some extra shifts. It's slow this time of year. He should be fine."

"What's up, Chief?" Darrell knew Seth well enough to know that he wouldn't take time off without a reason.

Seth thought fast. "I have a cousin on the Big Cypress Reservation getting married. Going to see some relatives I haven't visited in a while. Mom talked me into it. I wasn't going to go, but you know how moms are." Seth hated lying to his friend, but it was necessary.

"Yeah, I know, sounds like fun. Have a good time, and we'll see you when you get back," Darrell said. Stan was standing in the office and had heard part of the call.

The Alligator Dance

"Your lucky day, Stan. Seth is going to a wedding on the Big Cypress Rez, and you can have some extra shifts if you want them," Darrell said.

"Yeah, I do. Write me into the schedule. I'll take all you can give me." Stan was jumping out of his skin. He was pleased no one would be watching over him for a few days. Stan had plans, and they didn't involve being a park ranger forever. He hurried outside, and Darrell saw him talking on his cell phone.

Darrell laughed, "Couldn't wait to tell the missus, I guess." Over the past few weeks, Stan had been making more and more personal calls. Darrell assumed that Stan's new wife, Julie, had him wrapped around her little finger. Julie would be thrilled to know that Stan was picking up more hours as that would mean more money for the newlyweds.

The Alligator Dance

Chapter Fifty-two

The traffic to Tampa was moving along well that morning. Seth made it in good time and walked into the FWC office just after 8:00—a bit nervous. He read the wall by the elevator for directions to Captain Jacobs' office.

The door was open, and an older man with gray hair and a beard to match sat behind the desk. Seth rapped on the door frame. "Hello, I'm Ranger Seth Grayson. Liz Corday spoke to you."

"Hi, Seth, come on in," Jacobs said—rising and ushering Seth in. "She told me you were coming. Liz has been telling us your idea about going undercover at this alligator farm in Myakka. I was against it at first. They're bad people, but we need to have enough information to shut them down. We do have our own undercover agents, but since she recommended you, I'm willing to give you a chance to take these guys down."

"I know there's a genuine risk, but I want to do this."

"They're damaging the local ecosystem. There are RICO charges that could be filed for taking part in an organized criminal conspiracy, which I have no doubt will follow. I've been in touch with the Attorney General's office, and he agrees with this," Jacobs said. "When are you meeting with the person who does the hiring?"

"I'm going to the gator farm about 1:00 today."

"That's good. I'd like to see you working on the farm. We need names. How organized are they? Who are they selling to in Louisiana?" Jacobs said.

"I was surprised when Liz told me so much money is involved," Seth said.

"You probably don't know the half of it," Jacobs said. "We made a case where the state put out a bid for the rights to gather eggs in one of the wildlife management areas. A collector won the bid for $45 an egg. Plus they had to pay the state a $2.00 fee for each egg."

"Wait. You said 45 bucks an egg?" Seth dropped his Stetson.   "Yeah. When done properly, the state wins, and the collector wins. The problem comes when they collect more eggs than they report and pay for," Jacobs said.

"I understand the problem better now," Seth said.

The Alligator Dance

"Liz told me that you might be interested in becoming an FWC officer. Is that right?" Jacobs asked, focusing on Seth from head to toe, all of a sudden.

"Yes, Liz did mention it, and I've been giving it some thought," Seth said, leaning back in his chair and crossing his leg over his knee. "What qualifications would I need? It's just a maybe right now."

Jacobs reached across his desk and handed Seth some pamphlets. "These will help you make up your mind. From what Liz says, we'd be happy to have you apply. We need more people with interest in protecting Florida's environment and all who live here."

"Thanks for your confidence. Liz urged me to consider becoming an FWC officer, and maybe it's time for me to move. I've been a park ranger for a few years now. Since I've been working with Liz, I've learned more about what the FWC does. Seeing the poaching and how it affects more than just wildlife, I'm thinking harder about it. Thanks for seeing me." Seth stood and shook hands.

"You'd better get going. You never know about Tampa traffic," Jacobs said. "One big parking lot out there."

The Alligator Dance

Chapter Fifty-three

Seth drove along the highway and over the Skyway bridge spanning Tampa Bay. Turning off on to SR 70, he followed the directions the recruiter Carl had given him over the phone. Finally, coming to a dirt road that dead-ended at the Peace River, he slowed down and parked in front of a large industrial single-story metal building. Behind that was a compound of smaller buildings. The whole property was surrounded by an eight-foot chain link fence topped with barbed wire. Seth pressed a button on the intercom, and a disembodied voice answered.

"Myakka Gator Farm, can I help you?" said a stern, unhappy male voice.

"Hi, I'm here to see Carl about a job," Seth said.

The Alligator Dance

There was a slight humming, and the rusty gate screeched open, closing behind him as he stepped through. Seth saw more fencing and several hundred yards away, ponds with alligators of all sizes. He heard the grunting and thrashing of the gators. The air was filled with the rancid smell of the stale water and alligator shit.

A man in disgustingly-dirty blue overalls came out. "Follow me."

The smell coming from the man was almost as bad as the air around them.

Seth tried to engage him in conversation. "It's some kinda place you have here." The man didn't answer him. "What's it like being with all these gators here?" Seth tried again. "How many y'all got here, anyway?" He was met with stony silence. They passed down a short hallway where he showed Seth into an office. "Wait here," he instructed Seth.

Seth had an uneasy feeling about the whole setup and could only hope to get out of the gator farm in one piece.

After ten minutes, Seth got bored sitting in the hard metal chair and walked around the office. A laptop computer sat closed in the middle of the desk, surrounded by official-looking papers. He knew better than to touch anything right now. Pictures of alligators and their nests were nailed on the walls. A couple of rusted file cabinets lined one side of the office. In one corner, a white lab coat hung on a hook with well-worn dirty rubber boots below. He returned to his chair just as a man came in.

"Hello, I'm Etienne Fortier. The farm is my operation." Fortier took a seat behind a scratched and worn wooden desk. Wire-rimmed glasses perched on his nose. His hair was neat and stylishly cut. Lighting a slender cigar, the man relaxed, tipping the chair back. Seth was no judge of fashion, but he knew he would never be able to afford the clothes Fortier was wearing. The boots he propped up on the desk were alligator. This plebian man would be at home in the Columbia Restaurant, corner table, in Ybor City. Etienne Fortier was running the operation and letting everyone know it by his manner and the way he dressed.

Seth stood to greet him. He hesitated. "I'm Seth Billie. Carl said there might be a job for me here." Seth used a Seminole surname. He worried about giving out his real last name. They'd likely run a check on him.

Fortier stared at him for a long minute, making Seth very uncomfortable. Did Fortier already suspect him?

"You're a Seminole; am I right?" the man asked, still staring at Seth. He had a heavy Lousiana accent that Seth found hard to understand. Cajun, Seth guessed.

"Yes, I grew up on the Hillsborough and Big Cypress reservations," Seth answered.

"You have a white man's eyes, strange that," Fortier said, lifting his head and tilting it to the side, studying Seth.

The Alligator Dance

"Ever do any alligator wrestling? I hear the Seminoles are good at that."

"Just sport for the tourists a few years back. Some still do at places like Gatorland down by the Glades." Seth was now very uncomfortable at the way the conversation was going. Fortier gave Seth a creepy feeling.

"We can use a man like you. We gather gator eggs for the farm. When the gators are large enough, we harvest the hides and the meat. It's a business, and everyone makes money. I'll put you with Carl in the morning. Do whatever he wants you to do. We'll see how you work out."

"What time should I be here?"

"Be here at 5:00 in the morning, or you don't have a job. Wait outside the gate. Carl will pick you up there."

Seth had the job. Helping poachers rob from nests left a bad taste in his mouth, but he knew he had to make them trust him enough to let him work at the Myakka Gator Farm.

The Alligator Dance

Chapter Fifty-four

Leaving the farm, all he could think about was seeing Liz when he got home. He retraced his route back down to Sarasota and home. His mood lightened by the time he pulled into his yard. Seth's reluctance to help poachers raid the nests had almost faded into the background.

Nokosi hurtled off the porch to greet him as he turned off the engine and opened the door. Nokosi was trying to climb up on his lap. Pushing the heavy dog down, he said, "Whoa, pal, let me get out, will ya?" Nokosi backed off and followed Seth up the steps.

Liz came out of the kitchen door, drying her hands on a towel. "I'll have some supper ready for you after your shower," she called to him. "I can smell you from here. You

The Alligator Dance

been swimming with those gators?" She laughed at the big silly grin on Seth's face as he ran up the steps.

Catching her by surprise, Seth lifted her off her feet, swung her around, and planted a passionate kiss on her warm, full lips. "I needed that," Seth said when he finally released her and set her back on her feet.

She raised a hand and held it to his cheek, "I needed that, too. I was so worried about you. Go take your shower, and you can tell me all about your day."

Seth padded down the hallway. Nokosi lay by the bathroom door while he showered. Hearing the dog at the door, Seth had a feeling that his old pal knew something was up. Nokosi worried about him as much as Liz did.

Liz was putting food on the table when Seth walked in. The smell of fried chicken reminded him: he had not eaten anything all day. Liz had homemade potato salad, coleslaw, and fresh rolls. A pitcher of cold iced tea sweated in the middle of the table.

He saw a surprise on the counter, "Is that a fresh apple pie?"

"I hope you like it. It's been awhile since I've done much baking," Liz smiled.

"You know I'd love you even if you couldn't cook," Seth said with a smile—filling his plate.

The Alligator Dance

"And I guess I'd love you even if you were not trying to be such a brave idiot," Liz said, smiling back at him. They raised their glasses of iced tea and saluted each other.

The Alligator Dance

Chapter Fifty-five

Liz startled as a flash of lightning blazed across Florida's evening sky. A dark cloud shelf had come across on the sea breeze from the gulf. A crashing roll of thunder arrived a couple of seconds after. Even Nokosi ducked for cover under the kitchen table.

"This is going to be a good one," Seth said, beginning to clear the table.

"There is nothing good about this," Liz said, cringing as another crash of thunder followed an explosion of lightning. She hurried to help with the cleanup. Another crash of thunder made her jump, and a plate hit the floor.

Stooping to pick up the pieces of broken crockery, she apologized. "I'm so sorry. I hope that wasn't a family heirloom."

The Alligator Dance

Seth took the pieces and dropped them in the rubbish bin. "Don't worry about it. It's from Walmart and replaceable. Forget about the dishes for now. Come on," Seth said, taking Liz by the hand.

Moving to the couch, Seth held Liz tightly to stop her trembling. "It will be over soon," Seth told her, brushing the hair from her misty eyes.

"I wish I didn't let these storms get to me. I've lived here all my life, but I just can't get used to them," Liz said.

"I kinda like you being afraid. It gives me a reason to hold you close."

"I'd let you hold me close even without a storm outside, scaring the pants off me."

Liz obviously didn't know how much he wanted to get her pants off. Her warm body next to his was driving him crazy. He tilted her head up and kissed her gently at first.

A storm was raging inside Seth. How far could he go? Her response answered that question. Liz slipped her hand inside his shirt and ran her hand over his chest. Seth's arousal was getting painful. He had to stop this. He pulled her hand from inside his shirt.

"Liz," he whispered. "You know I want you."

Liz didn't answer. She calmly took his hand, pulling him off the couch, and led him down the hall to his bedroom. Standing by his bed, Liz kissed him passionately, deeply. Seth was lost in his desire for her. Liz pushed him onto the

The Alligator Dance

bed, unzipped his jeans as a crescendo of lightning and thunder rattled the small house. Kissing Seth, she knew she was ready to trust again. Seth moaned, ready to give her his heart and soul.

It was still pitch dark when Liz reached out and found that Seth was not in bed. She picked up her phone and saw it was only 6:00 am. Knowing she wouldn't be able to go back to sleep, Liz swung her legs over the side, toes feeling Nokosi's soft fur as he slept beside the bed.

"OK, dog, time to get up," Liz whispered. Bruised and sore from their adventurous lovemaking the night before, she moved slowly to the kitchen. Seth had left a printed note on the counter beside the coffee maker.

Liz,

I didn't have the heart to wake you before I left. The coffee is fresh this morning. Please let Nokosi out before you go and make sure he has water. I'll try and be back tonight.

I meant what I said last night.

Seth

Liz sat slowly in a chair, and a tear dripped down her cheek. Her tears were not from regret about the night before; they were tears of joy. A lightness filled her heart. At the same time, she was worried that Seth would get into trouble. What he was doing was dangerous, and he could be hurt, or God forbid, even killed.

The Alligator Dance

Nokosi planted his massive head on her knee and looked up with his soulful eyes that said he understood her pain and worry.

"Oh Nokosi, I love him, too," she cried softly, rubbing the dog behind his ears. His expression was one of sheer ecstasy. Liz smiled and bent down, kissing the top of Nokosi's head.

"I have to go to work. You go do your thing, and I'll get dressed," Liz said, letting the dog out. She poured herself a coffee, added milk and sugar, and brought it with her to get showered and changed. Looking in the mirror, Liz wondered if she looked different this morning. She sure felt different, lighter, more alive than she had in a very long time.

The Alligator Dance

Chapter Fifty-six

Seth parked at the gator farm gate a few minutes early. Four men drove up and parked. They apparently knew each other because they spoke in a little group a couple of yards away in whispers so he couldn't hear them. One nodded to him but didn't come over. They occasionally glanced in his direction. He could tell they were talking about him.

A dust cloud announced the arrival of Carl in his pickup. The four men didn't waste any time and climbed in the back, with Seth squeezing in by the tailgate. The truck turned around and bounced back down the dirt road. Farther along, Carl stopped by a small dilapidated house, and a portly man with sunglasses came out and hopped in the front with Carl.

The Alligator Dance

Before long, Carl pulled over, and the men began to jump off. Each grabbed a white tray. Seth was glad they had not gone back to the Manasota State Park—just in case he ran into Stan or Darrell. Carl came around from the front with the other man.

Seth couldn't help thinking that this Dr. Melendez looked a lot like the description of the man the college kids had run across in the park. Things were coming together and not in a good way.

The Alligator Dance

Chapter Fifty-seven

"OK, you all know the drill. Dr. Melendez is here to supervise the collection of the gator eggs. You have two hours. Walk along the river and find as many nests as you can. You'll be paid for each egg you collect. If you're not here when I get back, you'll have a long walk. Keep an eye out for the damn FWC and any park rangers or tourists. We are pretty far from the main activity, but stay alert. If you are caught, you know nothing. Understand?" Carl growled. "We don't come and bail anyone out."

"What are you standing here for? Move your asses," Carl shouted.

The men all grabbed their trays, spacing out along the river.

Seth picked up his trays and followed the others down to the river. Melendez was splitting up the group,

The Alligator Dance

sending a couple of men north and the others south along the river.

When it came to Seth, the doctor stopped and looked him over. "I didn't expect to see a Seminole doing this kind of thing. I thought your people were into protecting the wildlife and making money in the casinos?"

"Even an Indian needs quick cash sometimes," Seth told him. "I spent too much time at the casino poker tables."

Melendez huffed and sent Seth to the south. "Ask for Hector; he will show you what to do."

Seth quickly caught up with his group and asked. The men pointed to a short, dark Spanish fellow with a scruffy beard and drooping mustache.

"Are you Hector?" Seth asked.

"Si," Hector said reluctantly.

"The doctor said you would show me what to do."

"You know what an alligator nest looks like?" Hector asked.

"Kinda," Seth said, not wanting to give too much away.

"Come, I show you," Hector said and trudged down the river bank. He stopped by a mound of sand, grass, and vegetation. "Before you open a nest like this one, you look for momma alligator. Sometimes she hides, and you not see her. Always have your eyes on the water. Never turn your back. Momma can grab you and drown you before you can

The Alligator Dance

scream for help." Hector was thinking of another young man. A young man who maybe did not keep his eye out for momma gator and watch the water.

Seth cast his eyes over the dark water. Alligators were resting on the other side of the river. The sun was beginning to color the sky yellow then purple, and he wished he was any place but there.

"You dig careful, with your hands, so you don't break the eggs. Put the eggs in the tray. Use some of the nest to cover the eggs to keep them warm and move to the next nest. *Entender?*"

"*Si*," Seth replied in Spanish, "I understand."

Hector nodded, pleased that Seth knew Spanish. *Un poquito.* He would also watch what he said in front of this gringo. He thought back to Landon, the young man who had disappeared. Hector knew that momma alligator had killed him, left him in pieces.

"Hector, can I ask where are we?"

"This is the Peace River. There is a campground upriver. How you say? A preserve," Hector answered him.

Seth was confident that this was the same outfit that had raided nests in his park. The description of the man with the sunglasses fit Melendez. The fact that they were once again poaching on protected land was no coincidence. He hated having to collect the gator eggs, but he had to follow along and find out as much about the operation as possible if he was going to stop the poaching.

He worked close to Hector, digging up eggs from several nests, always watching the water for momma. Hector was working up ahead. Suddenly, Hector screamed. Running up, Seth found the old man on the ground, clutching his hand. Two deep gashes bled side by side on the fatty part of his hand near his thumb. The pain from the bite was excruciating.

"*Serpiente*," Hector moaned, pointing towards the bank.

Seth caught the tail of a water mocassin slithering into the river. Snakes often helped themselves to eggs— regularly eating the small gator hatchlings. The mocassin poison is hazardous because it is an anti-coagulant and causes unstoppable bleeding in the affected area. The toxin can spread through the whole circulatory system. The victim could bleed to death externally or internally, depending on where the victim was bitten.

"Shit," Seth knew help was a long way off. He tore a strip of cloth off his shirt and tied it above the bite. He'd been a ranger for three years but never attended a snakebite victim. Pulling out his phone, Seth hoped for a signal, turning around a couple of times and lifting his phone high above his head before he was able to get one.

The Alligator Dance

Seth didn't even think about the consequences and dialed 911. He could only tell them approximately where he was and that he would meet EMTs on the road. Helping Hector to his feet, he steadied him for the trek back out to the dirt road.

Hector protested, "The eggs. I must have the eggs."

"Fuck the eggs. Your life is more important." Seth worried as he half carried Hector to the road. The older man was fifty pounds heavier than Seth and almost dead weight. It took precious minutes to find their way back, and Hector was in lousy shape. He could be in shock, with unknown internal bleeding. Seth sat the man down and called Carl.

"What do you mean you called an ambulance? You dumb asshole," Carl shouted. "Dr. Melendez could have taken care of it. He could have cut it and sucked out the poison."

Seth was livid. "That only works in the movies. This man needs anti-venom and hospital care." Seth couldn't understand how some people could be so insensitive to another human being.

"I don't care what he needs. Just get those eggs back here and make sure that old geezer doesn't say a word about why he was out here," Carl shouted. "I'm coming out to pick you guys up. Collect the eggs and your trays in case they send deputies out to investigate."

The Alligator Dance

Carl hung up, then dialed his boss, who was not at all pleased. Next, he called Dr. Melendez to get the hell out of there, that he would pick them up as soon as he could.

Carl arrived first and picked up his men, ranting and raving at how pissed off he was. Melendez was useless. He didn't even look at Hector. Seth checked Hector's pulse and breathing and told the doctor that he was worried.

"Look, you're a doctor. Won't you at least take a look at him?" Seth asked.

Melendez turned his back on Seth and Hector and climbed into the pickup, tossing back, "He knew the risk."

Carl's tires spit gravel and sand as he tore off down the road as the wail of the ambulance echoed in the distance among the hardwood hammocks and sabal palms.

The Alligator Dance

Chapter Fifty-eight

The medics did what they could for Hector with a tourniquet, a couple of injections, and all types of monitors and transported him to Tampa General for treatment.

While they were loading Hector into the ambulance, he grabbed Seth's shirt and brought him close. Hector motioned for Seth to lean down so he could tell him something.

"*Gracias por tu ayuda, Seth, pero soy illegal*," Hector said as tears filled his eyes.

"*De nada*," Seth replied. He felt sorry for this man he had just met. When Hector recovered from the snake bite, he most likely would be deported. Seth hoped he might be able to do something about that outcome.

Seth watched the ambulance until it was out of sight and then realized that he was alone on the side of the road and didn't know where he was. It was a miracle that the ambulance had found them. He made one more phone call. This time he'd call Liz to rescue him.

While he sat and baked in the heat, he figured by saving Hector, he had put his whole undercover operation in jeopardy. Later he would call the gator farm and see if he was still employed.

Seth found an old oak tree to lean against and called Liz.

"You what?" Liz exclaimed, "You're where?"

Seth tried to explain where he was and hoped Liz could find him. He had one bottle of water left and was dripping sweat. The deer flies and mosquitoes were buzzing around his head, and the heat sucked all the air out around him like he was in a vortex.

He tried to plan what to say to keep his job at the gator farm. So much was hinging on that. Carl and Melendez were sure to tell that guy, Fortier, who seemed to be in charge of the poaching operation, what had happened to Hector and the part he had played.

Hector and his illegal status worried Seth. There had to be a way to help the man. Seth didn't condone illegals in the country, but he knew there was a human story behind Hector and wanted to help him any way he could.

He must have fallen asleep. The loud honking of the FWC truck horn made him jump. Pushing his hat up, he was happy to see Liz.

The Alligator Dance

"Are you for real?" Liz said, getting out. "This is the back of beyond. Where is this place, anyway?" She tossed him a bottle of ice-cold water.

Opening the bottle, Seth poured half of it over his head before taking a long pull of the refreshing gift.

"Thanks, I needed that more than you know," Seth said, wiping his mouth with the back of his hand, running the side of the bottle over his forehead.

"I think we are south of the Arcadia Peace River Campground. I heard them talking, and this is part of the nature preserve. These guys are breaking all the rules," Seth said.

Liz handed him another cold bottle of water. He wanted to drown in it but only took a few slow sips this time. "God, that feels so good," he added—climbing into her truck.

Climbing back inside, Liz cranked the air conditioning up. Seth directed the vents to hit him full in the face.

"Right, now tell me what happened here," Liz said, moving down the rutted road towards home.

"It's a mess," Seth said. "Carl brought four men plus me out here with this other guy. He said it was Dr. Melendez. He fit the description the college kids gave us. This doctor is supposed to be a research biologist. If he's any kind of a doctor, I'd be stunned. He sent me with Hector, who was to teach me the ropes. I can tell you, I hated collecting eggs from the nests. I had opened my second nest when I heard Hector scream. When I got to him, he was lying down in terrible pain from a water moccasin bite to his hand."

"My God," Liz exclaimed.

"I couldn't believe it—a snake bite," Seth continued.

"I know my mom is going to have something to say about this. There has to be a snake myth in this somewhere."

"What did the rest of the men do?"

"They were no help whatsoever. I called the ambulance first to get help out here fast. Then I called Carl. He was so pissed off and came out to pick up his men. Carl called Melendez to get the hell out of there. They took off and left Hector and me there by the side of the road. That so-called doctor was worthless and took off, too."

"What did you expect? Warm fuzzy hugs for saving one of their own? It was not going to happen, the bastards."

"I know you're right, but....," Seth had never come across people who had no human compassion, and it was a hard thing to understand.

They were almost home and turning on to Clark Road. It was late in the afternoon, and Seth had not eaten all day.

"Can you stay over? I'll order a pizza. We need to find out if I'm still employed by the gator farm and go from there," Seth said.

The Alligator Dance

"Sounds good. I'm not into fighting the traffic back to Tampa tonight."

Seth and Liz spent a quite evening discussing the problems ahead.

The Alligator Dance

Chapter Fifty-nine

Stan was sitting behind the desk when Darrell arrived at the station in the morning.

"Hey there, Stan. You're here early," Darrell said.

"Thought I'd get a jump on things, what with Seth gone and all," Stan replied. "Hey, I was listening to the news. A guy was bitten by a snake up on the Peace River yesterday. They didn't say what he was doing there."

"Good fishing along there," Darrell said, absently hanging his hat on the peg by the door.

"Yeah, you're probably right," Stan answered, looking down, studying his fingernails.

"I miss Seth," Darrell said, picking up the empty coffee pot. Seth always had a fresh pot brewing in the morning. Stan liked to be waited on.

Not looking up, Stan asked, "Have you heard from him? That wedding came up pretty fast. Julie and I sent out invitations six weeks before the wedding. It's strange he didn't book the time off sooner."

"You want to get out of that chair so I can do some work?" Darrell said. He was wondering why Stan was curious about where Seth was and when he was coming back. Stan should be happy to have Seth away because he was getting extra hours.

Stan got up and leaned against one of the file cabinets.

"Guess the Seminoles do their weddings differently."

"They must," Darrell answered. He had some reports to finish up, and Stan was annoying him with all the questions. "Why don't you take the Jeep and ride out to Gator Hollow? Check on the alligator nests. See if the poachers have returned. The eggs will be hatching soon if the poachers have left us any." Darrell figured that was one way of getting Stan out of his hair for a while. If he wanted to, he could have had Stan walk the trail to Gator Hollow, but it was too hot, and Darrell was not that mean.

"Seth is pretty tight with that FWC officer. Has she any leads on who the poachers might be?" Stan took his hat off the peg.

Darrell was tired of all the questions, "Look, why don't you ask him when he gets back? All I know is that Officer Liz Corday is babysitting Seth's dog while he's away."

The Alligator Dance

"Is that right? When is he coming back?"

"How should I know? The two of them have been running around asking questions. They think the poaching might have something to do with that alligator farm up in Myakka. Now get the hell out of here and go check out Gator Hollow for any more evidence of poaching. You're pissing me off with all your questions."

Stan threw his hat on his head and opened the door. Darrell watched him take his phone out and tap a number. *Boy, that new wife of his must have him by the short and curlies. Thank God, my better half is not that needy,* Darrell thought to himself as he watched Stan jump in the Jeep and head out.

Stan drove out the gate heading down the trail through the prairie to Gator Hollow, knowing what he would find. Walking along the bank, he found nest after empty nest. There would be no baby alligators from those nests this season. Stan made another call.

The Alligator Dance

Chapter Sixty

Liz woke up and heard Seth talking on the phone in the other room. She quietly tiptoed in to stand behind him, resting her hands on his shoulders.

"It couldn't be helped," Seth said to the man on the other end. "Yes, I understand. I'll be there." Seth flopped back into the couch cushions and let out a loud breath. "Whoa, I still have a job," he said, leaning his head back. "That was so strange. This guy, Fortier, who seems to be running the gator farm, wants me to continue working for him. It looks like old Hector is a favorite of his, and he was pleased I helped the old man. The thing is, the eggs will be hatching soon. I don't know how long this poaching will be going on."

Pulling Liz down on the couch beside him, Seth wrapped his arm around her as she cuddled into him.

The Alligator Dance

Liz thought a moment and said, "You know there are all kinds of things wrong with that operation. If they are selling eggs to Louisana, the buyer is paying for them. They can't be reporting all that income to the IRS because it's from an illegal operation. That falls under the RICO Act. We need to prove that their numbers don't add up."

"I'll find out tomorrow where he wants me to work. I'll talk him into having me work at the farm. Maybe they'll drop their guard, and I can do a little snooping in Fortier's office."

Liz reached up and stroked the scars on his cheek. "Please be careful. You promise me you won't do anything stupid like getting killed or anything?"

"I wouldn't dare. My mom is counting on me bringing you for another visit soon," Seth said, smiling down at her.

"I love your mom already," Liz said, laughing. Seth had a way of making her feel safe and secure. It looked like the dog was enjoying the joke too. His tail was wagging his whole body, a smile on his furry face, tongue lolling out. He gave a loud woof and climbed up in their laps, licking their faces, making them laugh even harder. He was a ninety-pound lap dog.

The Alligator Dance

Chapter Sixty-one

Liz heard her alarm go off before the sun was up. She rolled over, searching the bedside table for her phone. Finally, managing to turn off the annoying alarm, Liz rolled back the other way and snuggled closer to Seth, enjoying the warmth and feel of his body next to hers.

"Don't get too comfortable. We both have jobs to go to," Seth said, pulling Liz on top of him.

"Well, this is pretty comfortable. Maybe we have time for....," Liz purred, rubbing her body against his.

Seth laughed, and against his will, he gently pushed her off. "You're a tease. We'll have to revisit this idea of yours tonight." He got up and walked across the hall to the bathroom. Liz admired his backside until he closed the door.

After they were dressed and had a quick cup of coffee, Liz gathered her things and headed out. "See you tonight. The captain wants a poacher update, and there are a couple of other things I need to finish. Paperwork. Ugh!"

The Alligator Dance

Nokosi wandered down the steps sniffing the ground around Liz's car.

"You looking for that, raccoon, big fella?" Seth asked the dog. "You sure heard something last night." The dog's pacing and growling had woken up Liz and Seth. Seth had gotten up and looked out the window, but he hadn't seen anything. He told Nokosi to go to sleep, probably a raccoon or an opossum. The dog obeyed but continued to growl softly for a while.

Liz kissed Seth goodbye and went to get in her truck. Nokosi stood in her way and refused to move. "Looks like he wants to go to work with me today," Liz said.

Seth came over and dragged the dog away by his collar. As soon as Seth let go, the dog ran back to block Liz and nudged her farther from the truck.

"What is wrong with you this morning?" Liz said, getting annoyed. She wanted to beat the worst of the morning traffic heading into Tampa.

"Wait a minute, Liz," Seth said, looking at Nokosi. "Let's check. He's doesn't want you in that truck."

Seth approached the vehicle slowly and glanced inside. "Aw shit," Seth exclaimed, taking off his hat and running his hand through his hair. "There's a huge angry rattlesnake sitting on your driver's seat."

The Alligator Dance

"Shit, do something!" Liz shouted. Nokosi jumped up on her and almost knocked her down. Seth ran back into the house and came back with a long-handled broom.

"Is it unlocked?"

"No, at least it shouldn't be," Liz said, throwing him the keys.

Seth tried the passenger door. It opened without the key.

Liz could only shrug when he looked questioningly at her. "I swear I locked it last night. It's a habit living in Tampa."

The snake aimed at Seth. Its rattle sounding loud in the confined space of the SUV. An eastern diamondback can strike a distance up to two-thirds of its body length. He figured the snake was a full six feet long, so its strike zone was about four feet. Math was not his strong point, but he hoped he was close.

"Liz," he called softly. "Open the driver's door carefully all the way and get back on the porch. Take Nokosi." Once the door was open, and he saw Liz put Nokosi inside, he opened the passenger door. Extending the broom and pushing hard, Seth managed to move the snake. The snake was a lot heavier than Seth guessed and was hard to move. The rattler bit the broom handle and held on, its fangs dripping venom. Seth managed to push the snake to the edge of the seat. Carefully leaning on the passenger seat,

The Alligator Dance

he gave one last push, and the snake fell out the driver's side door. Seth backed up and looked cautiously under the truck to see if the rattler had hidden there. To Seth's relief, it was racing off for the scrub brush beyond the fence.

Seth realized he had been holding his breath and remembered to breathe. Sitting on the ground to recover, he decided he would buy Nokosi the biggest steak he could find.

Liz fell into his arms, crying tears of joy. They walked back to the house and sat in the porch chairs. Inside, Nokosi howled and scratched at the door.

Seth let the big dog out, and Liz knelt on her knees to hug her protector. "I'll never doubt you again. You saved my life, Nokosi," Liz cried into the soft fur of the dog's neck.

Seth swept Liz to her feet and held her tight. "I could have lost you. What if that thing had been under your seat and had bitten you while you were driving? You could have crashed. You could have died."

"I didn't. I'm OK," Liz said. "We need to find out who did this. Someone knows I'm staying here. Someone wants us to stop this investigation enough to kill."

"Well, that someone had better watch out," Seth cursed. He kissed Liz gently and walked her back to her car. Seth checked under the seats just to be sure and sent Liz on her way to Tampa. He watched the dust disappear down the road, regretting that he could not be with her every minute to protect her.

With the large rattler around, he put Nokosi in for the day. Better safe than sorry. After that, he got in his truck, after checking it carefully, and headed out to the gator farm in Myakka. He was more determined than ever to get to the bottom of this poaching business.

The Alligator Dance

Chapter Sixty-two

Seth drove up to the gate of the gator farm. The fecund stink of decay and fetid swamp permeated his truck. The chain link fence was at least eight feet high and topped with barbed wire. The wire was slanted inward towards the compound. It was intended to keep something in, not to keep someone out. Most people didn't know that alligators were very good climbers, especially of chain link fences.

Pressing the button on the gate intercom, he heard the same disembodied voice he'd heard before.

"Yeah, What is it?"

"Mr. Fortier told me to come in today," Seth answered.

"Wait there."

Seth could hear talking in the background but couldn't understand it. After what seemed like forever—yet was only a few minutes—the gate creaked open, and he

The Alligator Dance

walked inside. He got a creepy feeling being locked in with badass poachers and a couple hundred hungry alligators. Dr. Melendez shuffled out of one of the buildings and saw Seth standing there.

"I'm looking for Mr. Fortier. I don't know my way around here."

Melendez pointed with his chin, "That building over there. Down the hall, third door on the left," he growled.

"You back to try and save more old Mexicans?" Melendez said, laughing as he walked away.

"Rude bastard," Seth said, shaking his head.

He entered a dark hallway. Voices again echoed. The door was partially open, and Seth recognized Carl's voice arguing with Fortier. "There's something off about that Seth fellow. Why would he stop to help a fat old Mexican he just met?"

"Who knows?" Fortier had lost interest in the conversation. "I'm just glad he did."

"Why? What's that greaser to you?"

"That's none of your fucking business."

Carl didn't let up. "And that snoopy Florida Wildlife officer. You said she called to make an appointment. Are you nuts? One look around, and she'll know we are selling more eggs than our gators can produce."

"I have someone who is taking care of her. She won't be bothering us again," Fortier said.

The Alligator Dance

Seth wanted to punch that someone, hard. It wasn't by accident that the snake was in Liz's car. Someone knew she was spending time with him. But who would do something like that?

"I hope so. We have a lot riding on this," Carl said, and rushed out the door bumping into Seth.

"Well, if it isn't the do-gooder himself," Carl growled. "Better watch your back. I don't trust you, and I'll be watching you."

The Alligator Dance

Chapter Sixty-three

"Come in, Seth," Fortier called out. "Take a seat." Fortier was sitting behind his desk with his expensive boots resting on the top. Seth wondered if it was to impress him that Fortier could afford alligator boots and fancy cigars. If it was, it wasn't working.

"I'm surprised you didn't fire me for not bringing back my trays of eggs," Seth said.

"I did think about it, but old Hector is a favorite of mine. He worked on my father's alligator farm in Louisiana for as long as I can remember." Fortier sat back and closed his eyes for a moment.

He sat up straight again. "When I was about nine, I was clowning around one of the alligator ponds and fell in. I was about to be dinner for this big ten-footer when Hector jumped in and grabbed me. He threw me over his shoulder and yanked me out of there. I'll never forget the sound of that monster's jaws snapping shut. Damn gator missed me by inches. That is why I'm so grateful you were there to help him. I don't believe anyone else would have."

"I don't know about that. Glad I was there for Hector," Seth said.

"I want to bring you into the compound to help with the alligators. We have to keep moving them around by size and sex. Otherwise, they'll fight and hurt each other. The hides are no good with a bunch of holes and scars."

"I'd like to know more about the egg side of things. How are they hatched, that kind of thing." Seth pushed his luck, but he needed the information to pass on to Liz.

"That may come in time. But with your background, I think handling the gators is the place for you right now," Fortier said, his chin resting on his steepled hands in front of him.

"Excuse me?" Seth said.

"Yeah, you're a Seminole. Wrestling alligators should be easy for you," Fortier said.

"I've never wrestled an alligator in my life," Seth said, not believing what he was hearing.

"I thought y'all did that. Never mind. I'll have one of the men show you what needs to be done."

Fortier made a call. "Carl, get your boney ass in here. I have a new man for you to work with." He leaned back again in his chair and lit a cigarillo. Blowing smoke rings, he

The Alligator Dance

asked Seth, "So, if you don't wrestle alligators, what do you do?"

Seth had to think quickly. "I got in a little trouble and landed in jail up in Hillsborough for a spell. I got out a few weeks ago. Finding a job that pays enough is tough."

Before Fortier could ask any more questions, Carl knocked on the door frame.

"You wanted me?" Carl said with a scowl aimed at Seth.

"I want Seth to help you with the gators. Show him the ponds. Put him on the evening feeding."

"You sure, boss?" Carl said. "I think...."

Fortier picked up a large staple gun and threw it at Carl, barely missing him. "Yes, I'm sure. Just do what I say. You're not paid to think."

Seth could almost see the anger steaming off Carl.

The Alligator Dance

Chapter Sixty-four

Carl marched out, and Seth jumped to follow him. Throwing open the door to the outside, Carl let the door go, and Seth caught it before it hit him in the face. Carl stopped with his hands in his pockets and looked at Seth. "I don't know what your game is, but I don't trust you. Saving Hector was a smart move if you wanted to get in with Fortier."

"I don't have any ulterior motive." Seth lied. He was getting good at lying, and he wasn't proud of it.

"Whatever. Most of the time, he's a bastard to work for. The rest of the time, he'd just as soon feed you to the gators. It's a lousy, dirty, crappy job, but the money is good, so don't screw it up."

"I'm not planning on being any gator's dinner. I'm here to do a job, that's all," Seth stood his ground. He could not let Carl intimidate him. He had to earn his trust, learning enough to help Liz arrest these men.

The Alligator Dance

Seth followed Carl to a shed behind the main building. The stench of rotten flesh announced what was in the darkroom. Carl flicked on a light. A blood-covered table along one wall and a large chest freezer along with the other. Rusty butcher knives and a couple hatchets and trays decorated the table. Seth's stomach roiled as he forced himself not to throw up.

Carl opened a walk-in freezer and called Seth over, "This here is gator food. We have a chicken factory that gives us the extra stuff they can't use. Sometimes we can pick up roadkill. We also mix in some gator chow, now and then. This here's why I don't eat chicken."

Carl pulled on bloody surgical gloves, threw a pair at Seth. With gloves pulled up to his elbows, Carl grabbed a bag of partially frozen chicken and threw it on the table. With a hatchet, he chopped the chicken into chunks about a quarter-pound each. "We feed the smallest first. There is another gator galley near where the big boys are held. For them, we can get cows and other dead farm animals."

"How often do you feed 'em?" Seth asked.

"Once a day. More if we have it. We have an abattoir that sells us leftovers, but it's never enough." Carl chopped up another chicken carcass—blood, and guts splattering the table and the wall.

"Don't just stand there like an idiot. Grab one and start chopping. We have to fill those buckets over yonder and

225

take them out to the pond." A dozen five-gallon buckets stained with chicken blood were piled under the table. Stacked beside the buckets were burlap sacks of gator chow.

Finished with his first chicken, Seth reached for a bucket. There were rotting pieces of chicken floating in a pool of dried blood. Gagging, he struggled again not to throw up.

Carl watched Seth turning pale green and laughed. "You're a wuss. You'll get used to it. I did."

Seth hoped he didn't have to do this too long. He let his mind drift while he chopped up more rotten chickens. He knew he had to gain Fortier's trust and get a look around his office. Stealing glances at his watch, he figured Liz would be heading to his house in a couple of hours. He wanted to see if she had found out any more information on this place.

"OK," Carl said, throwing the last chicken in a bucket. He added a scoop of the gator chow to each. "Now we take these out to the flatbed 4x4 and drive out to the ponds. This is only the first lot. We have two more ponds to feed before we go home."

Seth followed Carl out of the confining shed, thankful to breathe fresh air again—inhaling deeply to clear his lungs of the stench. They loaded the buckets, and Carl jumped in and started the engine. Seth had to hurry and get in the moving vehicle.

The Alligator Dance

Chapter Sixty-five

They bounced down a narrow dirt path to a building that looked like an airplane hangar. A dirt berm encircled it along three sides. Carl stopped beside a wide door and shut off the engine. Inside the building were three pools containing different-size gators. Each pool was built the same way—a dry area sloping to about two feet of water.

"These guys are all under eighteen months old. The smallest ones are this year's hatchlings. Make three piles on the dry deck of each pool," Carl said. "Once they are over eighteen months, they're moved to one of the outside pools."

Seth did as he was told. The alligators thrashed and challenged each other to get the food first. Some were taking the food right out of the mouth of the next little gator. They hissed and growled, fighting to get their share of the meager offering. After a few minutes, all the chopped up chickens were devoured.

"Carl, is this building heated? Or is it just me?" Seth asked, mopping sweat from his face with his shirttail.

The Alligator Dance

"Hot water pipes run under the pools to keep the temperature right. These alligators are worth a lot of money. Tomorrow I'll show you how to clean out these pools." Carl spoke in a monotone and glared at Seth. Carl didn't like the way Seth kept asking questions.

"You're a real nosy bastard, ain't ya, with all the questions?" Carl asked, looking at Seth sideways.

"I'm just trying to learn the job."

"Hum…Come on. Now we go to the big guys," Carl said, picking up the empty buckets and throwing them on the flatbed. Racing down another narrow path, they followed it out behind the hangar to a large pond area about an acre in size. Here, gators waited, ready to be turned into belts, pocketbooks, and shoes.

Carl pulled up to another small shed. When Carl opened the door, the stench was worse than the last hut. Seth followed him inside to another walk-in freezer where a couple of whole sides of beef were hanging from the hooks—along with some pig and goat carcasses. Laying on the table were dead raccoons and a couple of squirrels—roadkill for dessert.

"If you like to shoot stuff, you can come back here and shoot all the raccoons, squirrels, and rats you want to. No one cares, and the gators need the extra food," Carl said.

Slipping on a clean pair of gloves, Carl took one of the beef sides down—almost as big as him—and began to

The Alligator Dance

chop it up. "Wake up and start chopping. I want to get out of here," Carl shouted at Seth.

Seth had so many questions. He didn't want to appear too nosy or too curious. He knew Carl already didn't like him asking questions. The Myakka Gator Farm was the dirtiest, foulest operation he could have imagined. It didn't take a genius to tell that Fortier and his crew were only in it for the money and didn't care at all about the alligators or the people who worked there.

After the buckets overflowed, they loaded the flatbed again and headed out. Standing at the fence and heaving chunks of the meat to the alligators, Seth was amazed at the power of the creatures in front of him. They lunged and thrashed—each one trying to get more than their share. One jumped almost entirely out of the pond, showing six feet or more of his jagged body. He landed atop two smaller gators, who snapped but did not gain any beef.

"How big do these gators get?" Seth asked.

"We let them get to about six feet or so," Carl reluctantly answered—throwing the last of the meat over the fence. Turning, he stopped and looked at Seth. His gloved hands dripping blood on the dirt path. "You writing a book or something? All you gotta do is feed 'em. Come on, and I'm outta here for the day. We'll drive the four-wheeler back and be ready for tomorrow."

The Alligator Dance

Seth didn't argue. He wanted to get out of there, hose off, and back to Liz. He had tons of questions and hoped she had some answers.

The Alligator Dance

Chapter Sixty-six

Seth smiled when he saw Liz's truck as he pulled into the yard. Nokosi bounded off the porch to greet him. The big dog's tail wagged as he jumped to put both paws on Seth's shoulders, covering him with sloppy dog kisses. Liz came out of the kitchen door, wiping her hand on a towel and tucking a stray strand of hair behind her right ear. She laughed at Seth dancing with Nokosi as the dog licked his face.

"Looks like someone is making supper, huh," Seth said to his furry friend, holding his head between his hands and ruffling Nokosi's ears, to the dog's delight.

Liz came down the steps to embrace Seth. She backed away quickly, "A...yuck, you stink. You been rolling in roadkill all day?"

"No, but I might as well have been. You should see the stuff Fortier and his crew feed those poor alligators. I know the gators will let a big kill rot a bit so they can tear off chunks, but this was disgusting. A slaughterhouse in the worst way."

Seth took a sniff of his shirt and made a face, "Ooo, right."

Liz was backing away with her nose wrinkled. "I don't even want you in the house like that. Take your clothes off outside, and then maybe I'll let you in. But straight to the shower. Do you have a bucket to soak your clothes in?" Liz backed away more. "Maybe we should just burn them."

Seth stripped off in front of the porch. "There's a big five-gallon bucket right outside the back door. And don't even think about burning these jeans. They're my favorite."

Liz tossed the bucket down to Seth, shook her head, and sat in a porch rocker.

Seth stopped unzipping his jeans and stared up at her. "You just gonna sit there and watch me strip?"

"Yup," Liz said with a smirk, rocking away. "I'm enjoying this."

Seth was exhausted but couldn't help smiling. He laughed and started to hum the stripper song as he slowly undid his zipper and pranced around. Liz broke out into gales of laughter and applauding, joining in the song.

Finished undressing, Seth stuffed his clothes in the bucket. He dashed up the stairs and headed for the shower. Standing there with his head against the wall, enjoying the

The Alligator Dance

blast of hot water on his back, Seth thought about how his day had gone and how wonderful it was to come home to Liz and Nokosi. Being with her made all the terrible things he saw that day vanish.

Liz was bent down, checking her dinner in the oven. Seth came up behind her, and playfully grabbed her around the waist and drew her into his arms.

"Hmm, you smell so much better," Liz said, brushing his wet hair away from his sparkling gray-green eyes. Seth kissed her lightly and peeked behind her at the chicken cooking in the oven.

"That anywhere near done? I'm starved."

"Perfect timing. The chicken is done, and we have roast potatoes and green beans. If you have room, there is a chocolate cake for later." Freeing herself from Seth's embrace, Liz turned back to the stove. She took the chicken out, remembering to move it away from the edge of the counter, out of Nokosi's reach. Putting the bowls on the table, she told Seth to take a seat.

At the table, Seth said, "You have no idea the number of foul chickens I've chopped up today. I also don't know how long I'll be able to stay awake. It's been a tough day. I do have a lot of questions I hope you can answer."

Liz served iced tea and began to fill her plate. Seth cut some of the chicken and groaned. "You would not believe what I've been doing all day."

The Alligator Dance

Liz put her fork down, "Tell me." One thing Seth liked about Liz was that she was a great listener and gave him space to gather his words.

The Alligator Dance

Chapter Sixty-seven

"My first job was feeding the alligators. This guy Carl took me to this shed that had a chest freezer that was not freezing anything. Inside was about two-hundred pounds of almost rotten chicken."

"Chickens? Really?"

"The stench was horrible. I'm so sorry, Liz, but I don't think I can look at a chicken right now."

"That's terrible. I tell you what, eat what you can. That way, you'll have room for the cake. I can always make chicken salad for the weekend."

"Sounds good."

"Do you know what they'll have you doing tomorrow?"

"I don't know, more of the same. It's really disgusting. Carl already has his doubts about me. I've tried asking questions about the operation, and he didn't like that.

The Alligator Dance

He also didn't like that I helped Hector. Claimed I had an ulterior motive. Little does he know I do, but I can't let on. Lying is not in my nature, and it's hard."

"Let's just hope you don't have to be there long."

"Yeah, I need them to trust me enough to let me wander around alone." Seth filled his plate with the beans and potatoes.

After they cleaned up and fed Nokosi, they took their cake and milk to the couch to relax and talk about what Liz had learned.

"What did you find out about the Myakka Gator Farm business? Is it legit?" Seth asked.

"I talked to my captain. There are twelve different permits they can apply for. We pulled the permits, and the farm has what is called a closed-cycle. That means that they have to raise and produce their own breeding stock."

"I'm guessing that's not what they're doing."

"What an operation is supposed to do is collect its own eggs, incubate them and raise the hatchlings to a marketable size of five to six feet. All that takes about three years. These guys are stealing from the wild, doctoring the books to make it look like their own alligators produce the eggs. They may be selling the eggs or hatchlings to Louisiana harvesters." Liz stopped to finish her milk and take the dishes to the kitchen.

"How do we prove that they are doctoring the books?"

The Alligator Dance

"That, my darling, is part of your job. If you can count the female and male gators of breeding size, that would help. A ratio of twenty-five males to seventy females is about right. The environment also has to be the right temperature. If it's too low, the alligators don't breed."

"I think I can do that," Seth said. He thought of all the things that could go wrong if he showed too much interest in the poachers' operation. He hoped he didn't have to work with Carl feeding the alligators again tomorrow, but if that was what he had to do, he'd do it. It would be one way of counting the alligators. He picked up a small notebook and pencil and left it on the kitchen table for the morning.

"What do you have planned?"

"I'm going to pull a surprise inspection on them," said Liz. "The captain suggested it. Maybe if they think we're watching, they might make a mistake."

Seth jumped up. "I don't like that idea. You could be hurt if things don't go right, if the poachers get suspicious of your motives." He sat beside Liz and took her hand. "I know you are a dedicated law enforcement officer, but...."

Liz stroked his cheek, "You don't have to worry. We pull these inspections all the time. I'll walk around, take some pictures, check the temperatures on the incubators, things like that—all normal things that an operation would expect. Besides, you will be there. Just try to pretend that you don't know me."

The Alligator Dance

Chapter Sixty-eight

Seth was up before the sun in the morning. He didn't look forward to going to the gator farm and hacking meat with Carl again. But he might be able to get Carl talking about the operation. Seth's objective for the day was to count the alligators in the breeding group. His main goal was to keep Liz safe.

He arrived at the farm a little after 6:00—as the sun was just starting to peek over the palm trees on the eastern horizon. Carl met him at the gate.

"We got a busy day today. First, we clean out the pools in the growing-out shed. The new hatchlings will be coming soon. Then, we feed again." Carl stomped off without checking to see if Seth was following him. Before they got to the hangar, they were stopped by Dr. Melendez.

"I need Seth today. We are going to take one more run for eggs. They'll be hatching soon. This delivery is our

The Alligator Dance

last chance," Melendez said, shifting his weight from side to side.

"Aw, come on, I finally get someone to help me out, and you're gonna take him from me," Carl said, obviously unhappy to lose Seth, as much as he hated and distrusted him.

"Take it up with the boss. Leave the feeding and come with me," the doctor said and turned to leave. Seth shrugged, looking at Carl, as he followed Melendez. Waiting at the gate was Carl's old truck. In the back were three bleary-eyed men.

Seth climbed in and greeted the men, but they said nothing. Seth leaned back and closed his eyes. He must have fallen asleep because the truck coming to a stop jarred him awake. He was surprised to see that they had stopped at the road bordering the back of the Manasota State Park.

Cursing softly to himself, Seth jumped off with the other men. Grabbing a couple of trays, he followed them into the park and across the prairie. They walked to Gator Hollow, the haven for gators. Seth was horrified that the poachers were taking eggs from the park again, but if he tried to stop them, he would blow his cover. As he walked by the slow-moving river, another thought crossed his mind. What if Darrell or Stan came along and found him with the poachers? Right then, he heard a Jeep coming.

The Alligator Dance

Seth backed into the cover of the palmettos and scrub pine as the vehicle stopped. He couldn't see who was in the small truck, but he could hear the conversation.

"Hey, Carl, I thought you guys were working up along the Peace this week?"

"We did, but old Hector tangled with a snake and ended up in the hospital. That new guy was there and called the ambulance."

"Yeah, I heard about it on the news."

"The boss was not happy with the attention, so we're back here. You got a problem with that?" Carl answered the man.

"Naw, the head ranger is gone off to a wedding. I'll make sure I do the run out here. Hey, when do I get my money? I'm taking a big risk here," the man said.

"Did you take care of that snoopy FWC officer?" Carl asked.

The man laughed. "I left her a special present in her truck the other night. The snoopy bitch hasn't been back here. So, I don't know if she's alive or dead."

Carl's mobile phone rang, and he dug in his back pocket to answer it. He stepped a few feet away to talk. While he listened, he turned to look at the other man. Carl's expression indicated he was not happy with what he was hearing. Hanging up, he shoved the phone away and approached the man.

The Alligator Dance

"I've got news for you. That lady FWC officer is alive and paying a visit to the farm today to check our damn permits."

"Shit," the man said, throwing his hat on the ground. He pushed his sunglasses up and raised his head to look at the sky, thinking of a way to save himself.

"Mr. Fortier is not happy. He said, and I quote. 'Tell that incompetent bastard he better fix this or he's gator bait.'"

Seth heard the Jeep start up and drive away. He was sure he recognized the voice of the man who had been talking to Carl, but couldn't believe what he'd heard. There were more lives at stake here than he imagined.

The Alligator Dance

Chapter Sixty-nine

Rejoining the group, Seth got busy opening the alligator nests. His mind was on Liz and her visit to the farm in Myakka. He needed to get back there. The poachers could make a body disappear without a trace.

After an hour of destroying gator nests, Carl called to the men, "That's enough, let's get this lot back."

Seth followed the men back to the truck, passing sixteen open nests. If this kept up, there would be no hatchlings in the park this year. He knew not all young hatchlings survived. Alligators were cannibalistic and would eat young gators. Other predators like birds, bobcats, massive bass, raccoons, otters, and snakes could eat the babies. Only once an alligator reaches four feet could they possibly be safe. Then, bigger alligators and humans were a threat to them.

The Alligator Dance

Back at the truck, Seth watched the men load the trays of eggs into the truck. He hated this, but he knew it was the only way to get the poachers to justice. Melendez climbed into the front passenger seat. He was talking to Carl, but Seth couldn't hear what they were saying. Seth watched through the window of the truck's cab and could see the doctor's Panama hat bobbing as he talked, wishing he knew what they were talking about.

It was a long, hot, and uncomfortable ride back to the farm. Carl drove through the gates and parked beside one of the big hangar-type buildings.

"Take these eggs inside and be careful," Melendez shouted to the men. Taking his trays of eggs into the building, Seth saw a table set up with boxes. The boxes had dividers inside that were the size of an egg. Along one wall, there were a couple of egg incubators. Seth was positive there were not enough to hold all the eggs they had brought back.

"You there," the doctor motioned to Seth. "You can stay and help sort the eggs. Fill the boxes with eggs. Any leftover can go in the incubators. Don't drop or break any. Keep them right side up. If you turn them, the hatchling will drown before it hatches. We don't get paid for eggs that don't hatch. Be quick; they must be kept warm."

The Alligator Dance

The doctor stepped away to make a call. "Yeah, we'll have this load ready to ship in a couple of hours. What? Who is poking around? Damnit. Be right there."

The Alligator Dance

Chapter Seventy

"You," Melendez shouted at Seth. "I'll be in Fortier's office. Find me when you finish. That fucking bitch from the FWC is at the gate," Melendez said as he stormed out, letting the door slam.

Seth waited a minute and eased the door open to look outside. Etienne Fortier and the doctor had their heads together, talking. Shaking his head, Seth saw Liz come round the corner holding a clipboard and a bunch of papers. "Damnit, Liz," he whispered. There was no way he could run to stop her or get involved. It would blow his cover. *Please be careful*, he said to himself. He went inside and filled the boxes as fast as he could. The eggs were larger than a chicken egg; the leathery feel was weird—reminding him of snake eggs. They were both reptiles, after all.

An hour later, there were only a few dozen or so eggs left over for the incubators. Rubbing the dirt from his hands on his jeans, Seth hurried to Fortier's office, hoping Liz was OK.

"I don't want that FWC bitch nosing around here asking questions and looking for permits we don't have," Melendez yelled.

"Don't yell at me," Fortier yelled back. "I didn't invite her. If that incompetent asshole had done his job right, we wouldn't be having this conversation. Maybe we need to find someone to do the job properly, eh?"

Seth saw Carl coming down the hallway. The crew boss knocked on the door frame and walked into the office. "I filled the boxes. Only about four dozen eggs for the incubators."

"Fine, you can go home now," Melendez said to Seth. The doctor was looking out the window, with his back to the room.

Seth didn't wait. He had to check on Liz and find out what she learned. Carl brushed past him, knocking him hard into the door frame on purpose. He glared at Seth, daring him to say something. Seth glared right back and left. He stopped outside the door, standing against the wall listening.

"You have to get this load on its way," Fortier said. "It's only a couple of weeks or so before they all start to hatch. Some even before that. We only get paid for the eggs on this trip. Take someone with you. Maybe that new guy. I want you to drive to Louisiana tonight, and don't stop. It's

The Alligator Dance

10-12 hours if you drive straight through. I'll call ahead. Tell them you're coming and to have my check ready."

"Melendez, I want that temperature in the van right this time. They also don't pay for eggs that are not viable."

"It's not my fault that other idiot turned off the heater in the van," Melendez said.

"It's your fault because you hired him," Fortier said. He turned to Carl, "Catch that Indian guy before he leaves. He can go with you this run."

"I don't like him. There is something off with him," Carl grumbled.

"I don't give a shit what you want or don't want. Take him with you, or else." Fortier fired back. "Now go get him."

Hearing that, Seth took off like a shot. He couldn't be caught listening. Seth also had a problem. He wanted to see Liz, but this could be the opportunity they were looking for. He had to go with Carl and find out where the eggs were ending up and who was paying for them.

Pretending to be ready to drive away, Seth saw Carl heading his way.

"Hey," Carl shouted. "Mr. Fortier wants you to ride with me to deliver these eggs."

"Sure, if I get paid overtime," Seth said, leaning his arm on the door and turning off the engine. "I'll have to call my girlfriend and let her know. She's expecting me to take her out tonight." Before he left, he wanted to hear her voice and know she was alright after visiting the farm today.

The Alligator Dance

Chapter Seventy-one

He took out his phone, found Liz's number, and pressed call. While he waited for her to pick up, he asked Carl, "Where are we going, anyway? She'll want to know when I'll be back. She's a bit of a ball-buster, but she has other qualities," Seth said with a smirk, keeping to the role he was playing.

Waiting for Liz to pick up was agony. Finally, he heard her voice, "Hello," Liz said.

"Thank God. I was so worried about you. I saw you today here at the farm."

"Are you coming home soon? I have so much to tell you."

"I can't," Seth told her. "I'm going with Carl to deliver a load of eggs in Lousiana tonight. Won't be back for a day or two, I figure."

"Aw...I'm not happy, but we can find out where the eggs are ending up," Liz said.

The Alligator Dance

"That's what I thought, too. I'd much rather spend the night with you than with stinky ol' Carl."

"Let's just hope you get there and back safe," Liz cautioned. "Call when you can. I won't get much sleep tonight."

"I will," Seth said. He was reluctant to hang up, but Carl was headed his way. "I'm coming. I just had to smooth her ruffled feathers." Seth jumped out of his old Ford and followed Carl back to the hangar.

Inside, Carl told him how to package the eggs. Each box had to be packed with straw to keep the eggs from moving. They carried the boxes out to the van. Carl wrapped an electric blanket on low over the boxes to keep them warm. A thermometer was placed inside one of the boxes to monitor the temperature. Once the eggs were secure, Seth and Carl climbed in and started off to Lousiana, a dozen hours and three states away.

The Alligator Dance

Chapter Seventy-two

Liz hung up from her call with Seth. She was disappointed he would not be coming home that evening but knew he needed to find out where the gator eggs were going, who was buying them, and how they could make the case in two states.

Unloading a few groceries, she put them away and turned on the oven to heat an eggplant parmesan frozen meal.

Putting Nokosi's food bowl down, she knelt and looked in the dog's sad eyes.

"I know, boy. I miss him too. He'll be home soon, I hope," Liz said,showering while her dinner heated. It was already dark when she pulled her steaming meal out and sat at the table. It was awful lonely sitting there at the kitchen table, so Liz took her plate to the couch and turned on the television. She watched the weather and was thankful that there was no thunderstorm predicted that night. Liz doubted

The Alligator Dance

Nokosi would be much help if she got scared. The big coward usually hid in Seth's closet until the storm passed.

She must have fallen asleep on the couch. Nokosi's chaotic barking woke her up. Shaking, Liz looked out the window. She thought she saw a shadow move across the yard and disappear, running down the road to a car half-hidden in the low brush and scrub on the other side of the road. The moon was rising but not high enough to provide much light. She grasped Nokosi's collar as she opened the door.

"A thunderstorm sends you into hiding, but you'll tackle a burglar for me, huh?"

Liz released the dog, watching Nokosi race down to the road barking. He froze there, looking before giving himself a shake and trotting back to Liz.

"Crap," Liz said. "Where is a big strong man when you need one? Come on, Nokosi. Maybe he was just trying to get into my truck." Liz looked back out at the driveway. "I hope."

Liz walked back inside, cleaned up the kitchen, and went to bed. Sleep didn't come quickly. Her mind kept flipping from Seth to the mystery man in the driveway. Was Seth safe with Carl going God knows where? What was that guy doing out there? And what did he want? Could she expect another snake in her vehicle in the morning or worse? She wanted Seth to hold her and tell her that everything was

The Alligator Dance

going to be OK. Liz settled for Nokosi. She called him up on the bed. She threw her arms around him and finally fell asleep with her face in his fur.

Liz was not ready for the alarm to go off at 5:00. Shaking Nokosi awake, she padded to the bathroom and ran the shower. Drying her hair, she heard Nokosi whining at the kitchen door and scratching to get out.

"Hold on. I'm coming," Liz called out to the dog. He rushed past her and hurtled straight to her truck, barking, and whining. "What the hell is wrong now?" Liz said, shaking her head. "Oh, please, God, no more snakes." She was tired and didn't want any surprises this morning.

Stepping off the porch, Liz crossed to her vehicle. "Aww," She moaned when she saw what was bothering Nokosi. Laying on the hood was a dead raccoon. Its throat cut and left to bleed out over her truck. The blood dried to black, dripping down the side of her truck. "Crap."

She didn't want to call Seth and get him upset. Instead, she put the dog back in the house, grabbed a plastic trash bag and a shovel. She managed to bag the dead raccoon and toss the body in a trash can, locking down the lid in case his relatives came to investigate. The hose washed the blood off her FWC truck. There was no way she was driving a bloody truck to Tampa, plus, she didn't need questions at her office.

The Alligator Dance

Someone was trying to send her a message and frighten her off. But who? And how did they know she was staying at Seth's house? She kept running up against more questions than answers. Rushing to get dressed and on the road to work, she missed seeing a man crouching in the brush across the way, watching her.

The hidden figure smiled and chuckled softly. "That should get the bitch running back to where she belongs."

The Alligator Dance

Chapter Seventy-three

Driving the hour or so to Tampa, Liz called her captain and briefed him. "I'll tell you more about the alligator farm when I get there. They have some permits but are claiming far more eggs than their operation should be able to produce."

"Good work, see me the minute you get here," the captain said.

Next, she called the park, "Hi Darrell, how are you and Stan getting on?" Liz asked.

"We're fine here. Except we had the poachers raid us again the other day. They got another bunch of nests. Stan was out that way, but he didn't see anything. They must have hit right after he left, go figure," Darrell said.

"Hey, you heard from Seth lately?" Liz asked. "I had a visitor last night at Seth's place. Someone left me a dead raccoon on the hood of my vehicle."

The Alligator Dance

"Jesus, Liz," Darrell said. "You think you should be staying out there all by yourself?"

"Maybe not, but someone has to take care of Nokosi while Seth is away. Do me a favor and keep your ears open. I have a feeling someone doesn't want me looking into the egg poaching."

"You could be right there. Do you want me to come out and stay with you a couple of nights until Seth gets back? Maybe my girlfriend, Marcia, could stay with you? I know she would love to meet you. I've been telling her about you and Seth and how you two have been getting along lately."

"That's sweet, Darrell, but I'll be fine. Nokosi is doing a good job of taking care of me. If he could open his own can of food, he wouldn't need me at all." Liz laughed. "Seth should be back in a day or so. How is Stan doing working full-time?"

"Oh, Stan is OK, and his wife has stopped nagging him. But he's still on the phone to her all the time. He's an excellent example of why I'm in no rush to get married," Darrell laughed.

"Well, keep me posted on any more poaching. Any eggs they left should be hatching soon. That's if they left any to hatch."

The Alligator Dance

Chapter Seventy-four

Pulling into the parking lot at FWC headquarters in Tampa, she saw Captain Jacobs striding towards the building. Liz quickly unbuckled, grabbed her briefcase, and hurried to catch him.

"Captain Jacobs," Liz called out to the fast-walking man. He stopped, turned around, smiling when he saw her. "I thought you might already be waiting in my office."

"I had a visitor during the night who put me behind," Liz said.

"Come on up and tell me about it. I'll get us some coffee," Jacobs said.

"There's a lot to tell," Liz said. She had to jog to keep up with the long-legged Captain Neil Jacobs. His office was on the third floor, and the captain took the stairs all the time. Liz always figured she was in good shape, but she was slightly out of breath when they reached the office. She fell into a seat in front of his desk.

Captain Jacobs reached into a small refrigerator and handed her a cold bottle of water.

"Thanks, I needed that. Looks like I need to hit the gym a bit more often." Liz laughed.

"That's why I take the stairs. Not enough time to fit everything in, is there? Now while we wait for the coffee, tell me about your visitor and what you discovered at the alligator farm."

The Alligator Dance

Chapter Seventy-five

"Hey, are we going to stop anywhere?" Seth asked
Carl as they barreled west along I-10 toward Lousiana. His
butt was numb, and he needed a pit stop soon.

"There's a truck stop ahead about fifteen miles or so.
We'll stop there to get gas and hit the head. My eyes are
turning yella. We'll grab something to eat on the road," Carl
said.

The miles they had traveled together had not
mellowed Carl's dislike for Seth. They had said few words
to each other since setting out that morning. It was now after
sundown, and Seth needed to stretch his legs. Pulling into
the truck stop, Carl wove around the eighteen-wheelers and
parked near a small diner.

Carl ran for the restrooms. Looking around, checking
to be sure he was alone, Seth pulled up Liz's number and
listened to it ring, praying she would answer. He had to hear
her voice.

The Alligator Dance

"Hello," Liz answered.

"Hello to you, too," Seth said, smiling at the sound. "I can't talk long. We are about halfway—somewhere past the Florida Panhandle. I lost track of what state we're in. Maybe Alabama. Carl is about as friendly as that rattlesnake we met. I'd rather ride with the snake."

"Great to hear your voice, dear. I won't keep you. I talked to Captain Jacobs today, told him all about the gator farm. Do you know where you are going yet?"

"No. Carl won't tell me where. We're still on the highway heading to New Orleans."

"Just don't do anything that will get you killed," Liz said.

"Believe me. I'll be careful. See you in a day or three," Seth said, seeing Carl approaching as he hung up.

The Alligator Dance

Chapter Seventy-six

Heading back to the van after a restroom break and grabbing a cup of coffee, Seth saw Carl on his mobile phone. His facial expression indicated that Carl was not happy with what he was hearing. He shut down the call when he saw Seth.

"Trouble in paradise?" Seth asked.

"None of your damn business," Carl growled, throwing him the keys to the van. "You drive for awhile." Carl shuffled to the back, opened the doors, and checked the eggs and the temperature. Slamming the doors, he turned to Seth as he crawled into the passenger seat. "I'm taking a nap. Wake me when we cross the Pearl River," Carl said, pulling his Tampa Bay Rays ball cap down over his eyes.

Seth started the engine. Carl was snoring before they were back on the I-10 and heading west toward Louisiana.

The Alligator Dance

They had been on the road for six more hours before Seth saw the sign for the Pearl River.

"Hey, Carl," Seth shouted, trying to wake his grumpy co-pilot.

"What, what," Carl mumbled, pushing his cap back up on his head. He rubbed his hands over his face and took a slug of cold coffee.

"We passed the sign for the Pearl River. It's straight ahead," Seth said. "Sign said *Bienvenue en Louisiane*. Must be close."

"Take the I-12, go straight at the junction."

"If I'm driving, shouldn't I know where we're going?" Seth asked.

"OK, We're headed to a ranch out by Covington. Funny, they call alligator farms ranches out here."

Seth followed Carl's directions, eventually leaving the highway. By driving the back roads, they ended up at the gates of Hightower Ranch. Carl got out and punched a code into the security box. The gate rattled open, allowing Seth to drive through. Following signs to the office, Carl ordered Seth to park and wait. The familiar stench of fetid water announced gators were close by.

"Don't you dare move or go poking your nose around. These guys will shoot you just for breathing. Personally, I don't give a shit, but Fortier does, and he signs my paycheck."

The Alligator Dance

Carl strode into the office and was gone a long few minutes. Long enough for Seth to see the same kind of setup they had back in Myakka. There were several hangar-type sheds, and he could make out a couple of large ponds packed with gators. Seth needed to get out and move after six hours sitting in the van. He was reaching for the door handle when Carl and two other men walked quickly out of the office building. One was tall, clean-cut, and carried a fancy silver-topped cane. The other man was wearing dirty jeans and white shrimper boots, carrying an extra hundred pounds, mostly around his middle.

"You know where to unload. I'll meet you there in a few minutes. After Arty here counts the eggs, I'll write you a check," the man said with a pronounced Cajun accent that was harder for Seth to understand than Fortier's.

"Arty, go with them," the man told his companion.

Arty was not a small man. It was a tight fit with three men in the front seat of the van. Carl drove around and stopped beside one of the sheds.

"C'mon, let's get this unloaded," Arty said, climbing out and opening the shed door. Seth found Arty's Louisiana bayou accent hard to understand as well. Seth stood back and let Carl direct things by opening the van doors and uncovering the egg boxes. Nothing was leaking. Good so far.

Seth grabbed a box and followed Arty and Carl inside. Rows of incubators lined the walls—along with two slimy, round, above-ground tanks with small alligators swimming in them. He watched Arty gently take each egg out of the box, check it over, and place it in an incubator.

As he did so, he tallied up each egg. Seth did some quick math and figured they had delivered over a thousand eggs. He was taking the last box out of the van. That's when the man they had met at the office rolled up in a golf cart.

The last box was counted, and the eggs were put in the incubator. The man turned to Arty, "Well, how many?"

Arty added up his sheet, "We have one thousand and thirty-two, Mr. Boudreaux."

"Very good," Mr. Boudreaux leaned on one of the incubators and wrote a check to the Myakka Alligator Farm.

The Alligator Dance

Chapter Seventy-seven

Seth had to get a look at that check. The number of eggs the poachers had gathered and stolen shocked him. Most had come from his park. Not all alligators hatched in the wild survived. Here they would all hatch and end up as purses, briefcases, belts, or shoes for those that could afford them. It made Seth sick to think about it.

Carl took the check and shoved it in his front shirt pocket. "Come on. We're heading back."

"Don't we get to rest or anything?" Seth said. He was exhausted and starving.

"No, gimme the keys. I'll drive for a while," Carl said, jumping into the driver's seat and starting the engine. "You just going to stand there?" Carl yelled. Then laughed, "You can always walk back."

Seth yawned, shook his head, crawling into the passenger seat. He needed coffee and something to eat.

The Alligator Dance

Chicory coffee and thin-sliced catfish or a shrimp po' boy would be good.

Seth fell asleep when they hit the I-10 heading east. He managed to sleep a couple of hours and woke up stiff and thirsty. Finishing off the last of his coffee, he watched the sky show a bit of light as they traveled east. They passed the Florida state line, drove three hours of nothingness to Tallahassee, more pine trees than people, and turned south down I-75 toward home. He looked at Carl. The check was sticking up in his pocket. He wondered how the man could still be awake.

Seth had an idea. "Hey Carl, can I take a look at that check? I've never seen a huge one like that. Must have a lot of zeroes."

Carl thought a moment, "Sure, why not. You can't exactly run away with it now, can you?" Carl handed it to Seth.

"Wow," Seth said. The check was written for over $70,000 made out to Myakka Gator Farm from Hightower Ranch. Seth handed the check back.

"Not bad for a couple of months work, eh," Carl said, laughing. "That's only one. We've had a couple before that."

"Yeah, but how much of that ends up in your pocket?"

The Alligator Dance

"Enough," Carl said. Seth could see the wheels turn in Carl's head. Up to that point, Seth didn't think Carl realized how much he was being used.

It was another couple of hours before they pulled into the Myakka Gator Farm. Carl pulled to a stop and told Seth, "You better come in. Fortier might want to see you."

The Alligator Dance

Chapter Seventy-eight

Melendez was leaning against a file cabinet when Carl and Seth walked in. Fortier and Melendez were looking at figures on the computer screen. Seth edged a bit closer. Fortier looked up. "How did you boys do?"

Carl dug in his pocket and handed his boss the check from Hightower Ranch. Fortier unfolded it. "Not bad. But not as good as before. The prices seem to have dropped again."

Fortier handed the check to Melendez. "Right, maybe Boudreaux is getting eggs from someone else."

Fortier rubbed his forehead. "I'll find out if he has any other suppliers."

Looking at Carl and Seth, he said, "Carl, you and the Indian here can take the rest of the day off. Be here early tomorrow. Any eggs out there will be hatching soon. You can see if there are any nests around our own ponds and go from there."

Seth walked out. He couldn't wait to get back to Liz. Getting in his own vehicle, Seth felt Carl watching him from the doorway. As he drove away, Carl gave him a wave. What was that all about? Carl hardly said few words to him during the trip, and now he waves him goodbye? Were they best buddies all of a sudden?

Driving back to Sarasota, Seth had an hour to think about the Lousiana gator hatchery, all the eggs they had delivered, and how criminals in two states had blood on their hands and huge profits in their pockets. Could Florida gators survive the onslaught of these crimimals?

The Alligator Dance

Chapter Seventy–nine

Seth's tires crunched the shell drive, alerting Nokosi. He was tired and worn out from his trip but anxious to see Liz. She opened the kitchen door, and Nokisi bounded down the step, almost knocking him over.

"Hi there, I'm glad to see you, too," Seth said, kneeling to give the big dog a rub.

Liz stood on the porch and laughed, her winning smile lighting up her face and warming Seth's heart. She jumped down the steps and ran for Seth.

Seth sidestepped his dog and took Liz in his arms and kissed her hard. "Girl, did I miss you."

"Thank god you got back safe. I was so worried. Supper for you, and then you can tell me all about it. I've got things to tell you, too."

Seth walked in. "Smells great."

The Alligator Dance

"Rolls are in the oven. I didn't know when to expect you. I made sliced ham, baked beans, and home fries. That way, it can be any meal you want. No chicken this time!"

"Mmm, perfect, I'm starved. I had one truck stop burger in the last twenty-four hours."
Sitting at the table, he reached across and held tight to Liz's hand while he ate.

Seth was too busy eating to do much talking. After supper, he helped Liz clean up and suggested they take their coffee into the sitting area.

"Oh, this is good," Seth said, sinking into the soft cushions of the couch with Liz cuddling beside him. "Another hour trapped with Carl in that van, and I would have gone crazy."

"So tell me," Liz said, tucking her tanned legs under her. "Where did you go, and what did you see? Tell me all of it." She had a lot to tell him as well but wanted to hear what he had found out so she could brief her captain.

"Carl and I packed up the eggs—cushioned with straw in the boxes. He covered everything with an electric blanket, and the temperature was monitored the whole time. We stopped once. That's where I called you from. It was a highway truck stop and where I grabbed that hamburger."

Seth stopped sipping his coffee. "Carl had me drive halfway. We ended up outside Covington, Lousiana. The place was called Hightower Ranch. There was this Cajun guy, Boudreaux. He had this big hulk of a man helping him named Arty."

Seth paused to draw her close for a long minute. "We unloaded the eggs into a shed with incubators lining one wall and a couple of pools jam-packed with small gators. Arty checked each egg and counted them. Next, Boudreaux wrote out a check and gave it to Carl."

"Did you see how much the check was for?" Liz asked, leaning forward in her seat.

"Yeah, on the way back, I talked Carl into showing it to me."

"Tell me, tell me," Liz said, bouncing now in her seat on the couch.

"You're not going to believe how much Fortier is getting for stolen gator eggs. Guess."

Liz threw a pillow at Seth to hurry him along.

"Over $70,000."

"What?" Liz screamed.

"That's right, 70 grand, and this was not the first trip Carl had made out there."

"Crap, this is bigger than we thought. No wonder...." Liz stopped and collapsed back.

"There's something you're not telling me," Seth said.

"I had a visitor last night. Someone left me a sliced up, dead raccoon on my hood."

The Alligator Dance

"What, Liz, are you OK? I should have been here," Seth said, jumping up, running his hands through his hair, and pacing in front of the fireplace.

"Don't panic. I'm fine, Nokosi heard him outside, and we almost got him. I saw a man's shadow. He ran down the drive and drove away."

"That's it—first, the snake and now this. Someone is trying to scare you off. Me too."

"I got that message. Who knows I'm out here?" Liz said.

"OK, there's Darrell. He knows you're taking care of Nokosi. Stan knows, too, probably. Did you tell anyone at work?"

"I had to tell my captain. But that's it as far as I know."

"Someone working with the poachers is trying to scare you off. I hate to say it, but maybe you need to go back to your place in Tampa."

"I will not. No one is going to scare me off. Besides, how are you going to keep working at the Gator Farm?" Liz fumed.

"You have to. I'll make it work. I can still come home every night to take care of Nokosi. I can't stand you being in danger from these idiots." Seth sat down beside her again, taking her in his arms and kissing her gently. He loved the feel of her soft full breasts against his chest—his body responding with a painful desire. The smell of her raspberry shampoo was intoxicating. He couldn't wait to get home to her each night. Now she wouldn't be here. But Liz needed to leave for her own safety. It would leave a hole in his heart until they could be together again.

"I'll leave in the morning. I want to brief Captain Jacobs on what you learned in Louisiana. How are we going to find who's been leaving me these awful gifts?" Liz leaned into Seth's arms, and then reluctantly pushing away, went to pack her gear.

"I'll call the park tomorrow, maybe swing by. See if Darell or Stan might have told anyone you were staying here." Seth went with Liz to her room to help her pack.

Liz went to the bathroom to collect her toilet articles. Seth was in the closet reaching to the top shelf for her extra duffle bag. They heard Nokosi bark and growl, racing to the kitchen door.

Seth looked out the bedroom window and saw one of the park vehicles pulling into the driveway. Nokosi was going nuts at the door, growling and scratching to get out.

The Alligator Dance

Chapter Eighty

Seth grabbed the dog by the collar, dragged him back to his bedroom, and shut the door. Nokosi padded to the bedroom window, front paws on the sill, growling deep in his throat.

"What's going on? He's so upset," Liz came out of the bathroom, her hand full of toiletries.

"It's someone from the park," Seth went down the hall to the kitchen door. He hesitated a moment and looked back at Liz, shrugging his shoulders, and opened the door.

The high beams of the vehicle blinded Seth as he tried to see who the driver was. The engine shut off, then the lights turned off, and the truck door opened.

"Hi, Seth," Stan called, cautiously approaching the porch. "I didn't think you were back from that wedding yet."

"I got back this afternoon. What brings you here?"

The Alligator Dance

"Eh… I was just checking on Officer Corday. Seeing if she needed anything. You know, it can be a bit lonely out here on your own."

Liz stepped out to stand beside Seth, gripping her duffle bag. "I'm fine, Stan. I'm heading back to Tampa."

"That's alright then. How is the poacher thing going? Any leads yet?"

"It's coming together." Liz was wondering why he was so interested. She had been at the house for several days now, and Stan had never checked on her before.

"Have you been up to the alligator farm in Myakka yet? They might have some information. You know, my cousin Carl works there. You might run into him when you do."

"Look, I have to let the dog out before he destroys the house. He doesn't seem to want you here for some reason." Seth was putting two and two together and not liking the math.

"Crazy, isn't it? Nokosi usually likes me."

"Yeah, right, maybe he smells a rat out here. You never know when one will turn up. I think I better let Nokosi out. He'll chase it down." Seth turned back to the kitchen door and put his hand on the knob.

"Wait, Seth. Maybe we should tell Stan what we found out. We don't want his cousin getting into trouble now, do we?" Liz said, hoping Seth would catch on to what she was trying to do.

"Right, why don't you come in, and we'll tell you all about it," Seth agreed.

"I can't stay long. The wife gave me a shopping list of stuff to bring home," Stan said, showing a note from his pants pocket.

"Not a problem. Come on in. Liz has a call to make, and then we'll both tell you what we found out." Seth and Liz could only hope that they were reading each other right. It had dawned on both of them that Stan was the one leaving the dreadful presents for Liz in the hopes of scaring her back to Tampa. Nokosi deserved all the credit for saving Liz's life and alerting them to the part Stan had been playing in all that had been going on.

"I'll make it from the bedroom and see if I can calm Nokosi down at the same time." Liz hurried to the bedroom and punched in Captain Jacob's number.

Seth offered Stan coffee and passed the time, telling him about the wedding he had attended on the Big Cypress Reservation. Seth was amazed at how good he was getting at making up stories and making people believe them.

After her call, Liz returned to the kitchen. "Sorry, I can't stay to talk. Captain Jacobs wants me in the office ASAP. We'll have to talk another time, Stan. I have to finish packing. Please stay a bit and talk with Seth."

The Alligator Dance

"Naw, that's OK, I better be going. Seems like everything is under control here." Stan suddenly found he also had to get out of there fast.

"It was nice of you to stop by and check up on me, Stan," Liz said, delaying his departure.

"How's that new wife of yours? You settling into married life, OK?" Seth said, playing along. "Darrell might be joining you before long if Marcia has her way."

"Julie is great." Stan was shuffling his feet, visibly anxious. "It's all good." His mind was losing interest in the conversation.

"Yeah. Thanks again for stopping by. It's good to know someone was watching over Liz while I was away. How were things at the park? Did you see any more poachers there?" Seth asked, stalling for more time.

"No, I didn't see any. I have to get going now. See you when you come back to work."

Stan was nervous and hurried out—jumping back in his truck. Seth and Liz waited until he disappeared down the drive before they went back into the house.

Liz ran to let Nokosi out of the bedroom. The dog raced out past Seth and flew out the open door. He stopped to sniff around where the truck had been parked. Looking toward the road, he growled and bared his teeth.

The Alligator Dance

"Nokosi, come back here," Seth called. The dog looked back at Seth and then barked one last time before padding slowly to the house.

A few minutes later, they heard the wail of a police siren and knew that Stan would be spending at least one night in jail, if not a lot more.

The Alligator Dance

Chapter Eighty - One

Liz plopped down heavily in a chair at the kitchen table. "I'm glad you figured out what I was doing."

Seth let out a breath and sat opposite her. "It dawned on me that Stan's been the one leaving you presents—hoping to scare you off. I'm not sure why he turned up tonight, but he was surprised I was here. I was going to call the station anyway tomorrow and let Darrell know I'm back. I'll take the rest of the week off from the park. Do you think we can wrap this up by then?"

"Have you given any more thought to coming over to the dark side? You know, working for the Florida Fish and Wildlife Commission as an enforcement officer?" Liz knew he would love the job and be good at it. "I know Captain Jacobs will vouch for you."

The Alligator Dance

"Maybe when this is all over, I'll look into it. One thing at a time."

Liz couldn't help thinking about the future. And how much she wanted to have Seth a part of her future. "I'm worried about Stan's cousin working at the alligator farm. What if his cousin Carl figures out why you are there? You could be in serious danger. Maybe even killed. I don't want to be without you." Liz reached across to take his hand.

Seth rubbed his thumb over her knuckles while looking into her dark brown eyes. "I'll be careful. Be sure your Captain Jacobs can make a case."

"Speaking of that, I'd better get a move on. I'm meeting Jacobs first thing. If you can find us some tangible proof, like that check you saw, records of deliveries to Louisiana? Anything that might help."

"I'll do my best. I don't know what that crazy Cajun Fortier will have me doing tomorrow. Every day is something different. I don't want to feed those damn gators again."

Liz picked up her duffle and backpack again. "This time, I'm really going. But you know I don't want to." She walked over to the kitchen door, hoping Seth would stop her.

He didn't. Seth walked beside her. Watching her throw her things in the back of her truckwas agony. He wanted her to stay. It was best she go now and brief Jacobs in the morning. Seth opened the door. Before she got inside, he wrapped his arms around her and kissed her gently at first. Deepening the kiss, he drank in the taste of her and wished the moment could last forever.

"Call you tomorrow," Liz slid into the driver's seat, fastening her seat belt. Taking one more look at Seth, she drove out of the driveway.

Seth walked slowly into the house. The house was empty without Liz. Nokosi lay on the floor with his head on his paws, looking very sad.

The Alligator Dance

Chapter Eighty-two

Waking up before sunrise, the thought of going back to the gator farm depressed Seth. He'd see it through and help put these poachers in jail where they belonged. He showered and let the dog out to do his thing. He had to be at the farm by 8:00 to find out his duties for the day. Taking his coffee to the front porch, Seth laughed watching Nokosi chase the squirrels around the old oak tree. It was warm and muggy, and he was sweating before long. His thoughts were racing as he headed back into the house. Finally, it was late enough to call Darrell.

Darell's phone rang and was about to go to voicemail when he picked up.

"Yeah, Who's this at this hour? It's still dark for Pete's sake?" Darrell grumbled. "You better have a good reason for waking me up."

"I do if you'll give me a chance," Seth chuckled.

"Hi, Chief. You coming back? Please." Darrell said, recognizing Seth's voice.

The Alligator Dance

"Back in town, but I need a few more days off to catch up. I have to ask you. How have things been going with Stan?"

"He's OK but spends so much time on the phone. We had a couple of small summer camp groups come in that I had him take around and give a talk to. He did alright, but I could tell he didn't capture their attention. The kids were bored. Not like when you do it."

"Did Stan say anything about checking up on Officer Corday?"

"No, why?"

"He showed up here at my place last night. Saying he was checking on her. There have been some strange things happening—like the rattler left in Liz's truck. The other night she found a dead raccoon on her hood. Nokosi went mad when he heard Stan drive up. That was alarming. Nokosi has never had a problem with him before."

"Wow, is she alright?"

"Liz can handle herself. Look, Stan got himself arrested last night on the way home from my place."

"What? How did that idiot get himself arrested? And how did you find out about it? You have some explaining to do, Chief."

"Yeah, I know. I'll tell you all about it later. Look, you're going to have to get a part-time ranger to fill in for a few days until I get back. We'll get together soon and catch up? I'll toss a couple steaks on the grill."

"Let me know when, and I'll be there. I'd never turn down a free meal. See you later."

Seth hung up, wondering what to think about Stan's visit. Was he indeed being the good Samaritan and checking to see if Liz was OK? Or was there something more sinister in his visit? Seth was betting on sinister after Stan said his cousin worked at the alligator farm. That did it for Seth. Stan just could not be trusted.

The Alligator Dance

Chapter Eighty-three

Seth headed off to Myakka. In the summer, when all the snowbirds are gone, the traffic was light, and he made it to the farm just before 8:00. After pressing in the code, the gate to the compound rattled open. Moving quickly to Fortier's office, he rounded a corner and ran smack into Dr. Melendez.

"Ah, the Indian. Come with me today."

"Sure, OK," Seth said. What would the doctor have him doing today?

Seth followed the doctor to the hangar, where they had packed the eggs for Louisanna. Most of the eggs in the incubators had hatched, and little alligators, no longer than six to eight inches, were crawling over each other. Cute enough at this stage to be a pet, then one day a predator. Even at this stage, they could inflict a dangerous bite.

"Your job today is to move all the juveniles in pool two to the outside. Move the ones in pool one to the now empty pool, and then all the hatchlings go over to that pool. We keep moving the alligators along from one to the other as they grow. Fortier said that since you were Seminole, you would be good to have around the gators." Melendez laughed.

"I've never wrestled gators. This is my first time working with them."

"I think Fortier's nuts," said Melendez. "But then, what do I know?"

Seth was slightly pleased with his assignment. At least he wasn't working with Carl feeding the big alligators their disgusting meal. Until Melendz said, "Then you can feed them."

"Oh, great," Seth mumbled, watching him leave the building.

Seth turned, putting his hands on his hips to look at the alligators. First, he had to move the larger ones out. The gators were up to three feet long and as dangerous as hell. They could easily take off a finger or hand.

He stood there a moment, arranging his strategy. Seth had to grab one gator without getting tagged by another one. He spotted a large plastic bin on wheels up against a wall and had an idea. Pushing the container up to the tank, Seth reached in and quickly grabbed a gator behind its snapping jaws. He dropped it into the bin. One down, a couple dozen left to go.

The Alligator Dance

After he had six alligators in the container, he rolled it out to the pond. That's where the juveniles would live and grow to over five feet. Then they'd be ready to be slaughtered and their hides sold to the fashion trade.

Seth was conflicted about the trade in alligator hides. He hated to see the animals killed so someone could wear the latest fashion trend. But it also meant jobs for so many people along the line. Legal jobs and, in this case, illegal. Besides, he happened to like fried alligator.

He came back into the building after putting the last of the juveniles in the pond.

Fortier stood there, looking at the empty tank. His obnoxious cigar was adding to the funk of the stale air.

Fortier turned when he heard Seth crashing the awkward container against the door frame and pushing it back inside. "I knew you would be the right man for this job. I can't wait to see you with the bigger boys." Fortier chuckled to himself as he left, enjoying an inside joke that Seth didn't get.

You got to be shitting me. Seth groaned inside. The sooner this was over, the better. He had to find a way to get into the office and see if he could prove that Fortier was getting paid for shipping eggs to Louisiana and who was buying.

He transferred the alligators from one tank to the next until he reached the small hatchlings. He opened the

The Alligator Dance

incubator and smiled at the little reptiles. At this size, they were so cute and not as lethal as their bigger relatives. Seth could pick up one in each hand so long as he watched his fingers. The little guys could still give a pretty painful and lousy bite and would hang on for dear life.

It didn't take Seth long to put the hatchlings in the tank where they could grow for a few months. Now all he had to do was feed them.

The Alligator Dance

Chapter Eighty-four

Carl was already in the feed shed, chopping up the rotten food for the outside ponds when Seth got there.

"I see you're making yourself indispensable with Mr. Fortier and Dr. Melendez," Carl sneered. Seth could feel the hate and distrust coming off Carl as he spoke.

"I don't know about indispensable. I've just got a job to do, and I'll do it," Seth answered back. Now that he knew about the connection between Stan and Carl, he had to be even more cautious.

"Hey, what about that FWC lady that was snooping around the other day? Anything to be worried about?"

Carl leaned back against a table, a big smirk on his face. "I know a trick or two about how to get rid of a pesky broad. We've already played a couple on her and sent her packing back to Tampa."

The Alligator Dance

"You mean she was staying somewhere local?" Seth was playing dumb to see what he could find out. He needed to confirm Stan's part in terrorizing Liz.

"Yeah, my cousin is a park ranger for the Manasota State Park. His boss was letting that FWC officer use his place while he was away. Some story about watching the guy's dog. Anyway," Carl stopped to smile and laugh, "I had my cousin pull a couple pranks on the bitch to scare her off. Looks like it worked, too. She ran off back to Tampa with her tail between her legs," Carl burst out laughing hard, turning back to the table to chop up some more smelly chicken. It was supper time.

Seth was seething, his fists balled at his sides, wanting to slap that grin right off Carl's face. But he had to keep up the cover story. Grabbing a pail, he filled it with scraps and took it back to the shed to feed his scaly charges.

Talking to the hatchlings squirming in the tank, "Hi guys. Hope you like what's on the menu today." He tossed small pieces of chicken into their little mouths. Even at only a few days old, they fought each other for the smelly scraps. In the wild, they would be cared for and protected by their mother. Here at the farm, all their care was solely by humans to raise them large enough to be killed. Seth wiped a bead of sweat from his forehead before it ran into his eyes. The shed was kept at 86 degrees and humid. Perfect for the alligators to grow to marketable size.

The Alligator Dance

Seth was developing a soft spot for the little reptiles, knowing what was ahead for them. He also knew he couldn't do anything about their fate now. Finished with the feeding, Seth picked up the empty pails and took them back to the feed shed. Luckily he didn't run across Carl again. He was in no mood for his wisecracks about Liz.

The Alligator Dance

Chapter Eighty-five

Nokosi bounded off the porch when Seth turned his old Ford into his yard. "Hi there, ol' thing. Ya miss me?" Seth reached down and ruffled the dog's fur as he climbed the steps. He had his hand on the doorknob when it hit him. Liz was not inside, waiting for him. He shuffled into the silent kitchen—no aroma of bread, chicken, something cooking. The table was not set with wildflowers in a small vase. Seth missed all the feminine touches Liz had brought to his life. He was starving, but nothing in the refrigerator appealed to him.

Nokosi was sitting at his side, watching him with baleful eyes. "Ya, ya, OK." Seth closed the refrigerator. He filled the dog's dish with Kibble and a half can of food. The dog looked up as much as to say thanks and dived into his supper.

The Alligator Dance

The sun had not set yet, and Seth knew the park would still be open. He decided to grab some fast food and check-in with Darrell. Calling the park, Seth reached a recording of the park hours. Hanging up, he tried to break the gloom. "Come on, Nokosi, let's go for a ride."

Seth arrived at the ranger station just as Darrell was turning the key in the door. The sound of tires crunching on the drive caught his attention. The ranger waved to Seth and walked over to the vehicle. "Hey, what brings you out here at this hour? I'm happy to see you, though. Sure missed having you around."

"I missed you, too. Did you manage to get someone to fill in for a bit?

"Yeah, I got a guy from FSU. He's taking a couple of courses this summer and needed the money. He knows it's not much. One course was in conservation, and the other was for his Bachelor of Science degree. His name is Dan Myers, and he passed all the requirements."

"Great. I look forward to meeting our new ranger. I wanted to see how things were going around here without me." Seth sat at the picnic table under the oak tree. The sun was setting in the west, and a breeze was blowing a storm in from the gulf. The birds sensed it and were on the wing overhead. Black clouds were building, and flashes of lightning sparked deep inside them.

The Alligator Dance

Darrell perched on the opposite side of the table. He took off his hat and looked at the darkening sky. "Looks like we're in for a doozy."

"In more ways than one," Seth muttered. "Look, I have to ask. Who knew about Liz staying at my place?"

"I didn't think it was any secret, but I didn't blab it about. Far as I know, only Stan and I knew she was staying there. Maybe her boss up in Tampa knew. I did mention it to Marcia. Why?"

As the first big drops began to splatter the table, Seth told Darrell about the rattler in her truck and the sliced up raccoon. "Liz has gone back to her place in Tampa. Someone's been trying to frighten her off the poaching investigation."

"Christ, Seth. You got any idea who?"

"Yeah, I do. Can you keep it together here for a few more days? I have some things to take care of. Do me a favor: don't tell anyone I'm back. I'm going to do some investigating on my own." Seth stood and called the wandering Nokosi back from chasing small geckos.

"I'll do whatever you want," Darell said, walking with Seth to their vehicles.

Over the hood, Seth called to Darrell, "I mean it, Darrell, not a soul."

The sky opened, and a torrent fell. Darrell waved to Seth.

The Alligator Dance

"Let's get some disgusting fast food and go home," Seth said to the smelly wet dog.

Seth drove to the neon lights of Tamiami Trail and stopped at the first burger place. He ordered a couple of burgers and fries for himself, a plain one for Nokosi. He ate as he drove, thoughts swimming around in his head.

The Alligator Dance

Chapter Eighty-six

It had only been a few days, but it felt like a lifetime. Seth missed Liz. He was going home to an empty house, an empty bed. Seth wanted what his parents had, a life shared with love and understanding. His head told him it was too soon, be practical, take your time, and get to know each other. But his heart told him differently. Maybe he would visit his parents on the weekend, if they managed to arrest the poachers and shut down the gator farm.

Nokosi stood up and barked as he drove into his driveway. Liz's truck was there, and the lights were on in the house. He ran through the downpour, racing into the kitchen and sliding to a stop on the wet floor.

Time stood still when he saw Liz walking down the hall, wrapped in a towel and drying her hair. When she saw him, her smile lit up the room brighter than a bolt of lightning. He took her in his arms. He kissed her passionately, taking her mouth with his and parting her lips, exploring its depths, meeting her tongue with his. He released the towel from around her, picking her up and carrying her back to his room.

Seth woke in the early hours—as the moon cast shadows across the room. Raising himself on one elbow, he watched Liz sleep. Her eyes fluttered open, and she saw him staring at her.

"See anything you like?"

"Yeah, as a matter of fact, I do." Seth snaked his hand under the blanket finding her breast. He stopped there; the feel of her in his hand was tender and amazing. His hand traveled lower. She was ready and waiting for him.

"You're a scoundrel," Liz exclaimed, throwing the blanket over their heads as she slid down the bed.

Later, spent and happy, Seth sat on the edge of the bed, not wanting to get up and face the day ahead. Liz traced the muscles in his back, running her hands up and down. She knelt up and bit his earlobe, calling his attention back to her.

"I thought we agreed you'd stay in Tampa until this was over."

Liz flopped back onto the bed, "I couldn't stay away. I tried, but my place was so cold and lonely. I thought about you all day. You're not happy I came?"

The Alligator Dance

"Believe me. I'm thrilled you came. I'm worried you could get hurt. I couldn't take it if anything happened to you," Seth turned and kissed her gently on her neck.

"Where are we going with this? Is this just a fling until we catch the bad guys, and then we go our separate ways? I've been hurt before, and as much as I'm enjoying whatever this is, I'd like to know," Liz said shyly, afraid, and hopeful at the same time.

Seth returned to the edge of the bed, staring out the window. "I can't lie to you, Liz. I honestly don't know. What I do know is that when you're not here, I can't breathe for wanting you. I've never felt like this with anyone else. I can only hope you will give us time to see if it's going anywhere."

"Fair enough," Liz said. She threw the covers off and shuffled for the bathroom. They both had dangerous jobs today and an illegal operation to shut down as quickly as possible.

The Alligator Dance

Chapter Eighty-seven

Over coffee, it was all business. Seth and Liz shared information on the alligator farm. Liz had researched how an alligator farm should be run. Everything from the permits necessary to how the reptiles should be housed and cared for. Each time, Seth was able to describe all the rules the poachers were breaking.

"We still need proof of how many eggs they are selling to Louisiana," Liz said.

Seth nodded in agreement, sipping his coffee. "I'll try again today to get into the office. Fortier must leave it sometimes. He's got this idea that because I'm a Seminole, I'm the perfect person to take care of the alligators."

"So long as he doesn't go asking you to start wrestling them," Liz joked. She was worried that letting Seth investigate put his life in danger.

The Alligator Dance

Seth didn't want to tell her that Fortier had already brought that subject up a couple of times. He just hoped the crazy Cajun didn't act on it.

Taking her cup to the sink, Liz told him, "I'm seeing my captain again today. I've been thinking that we need FWC officers to raid the farm. And we need to stop sending you in there. Anything could happen."

"If officers try to raid, Foriter could destroy all the evidence before they get through the gate. I'll get into his office today somehow. I'll figure a way to distract him and get the evidence we need. Then you can send in whoever you want." Seth helped to clear up the table and feed Nokosi.

"Maybe I could say I need Fortier to check on something in one of the outside ponds. That should keep him busy long enough." Seth was pretty pleased with his plan. Could it work? If he described it right, Etienne Fortier was just crazy enough to think it was his idea.

Checking his watch, Seth needed to get to the farm soon, and Liz had to fight the traffic on I-75. They didn't want to leave each other, but the sooner they parted, the better for what each faced today. Liz gathered her things, and they walked out together. Seth checked both vehicles for unwanted visitors. It was a habit now. Seth opened the door for Liz and waited while she turned on the engine and buckled her seatbelt.

The Alligator Dance

"You be careful, please. I have plans for you later," Liz said with a wink and a grin.

"You better believe it. If you're free this weekend, I want to see my folks. I'd like you to come. My mom will be over the moon if you do."

"I think your mom is matchmaking," Liz said.

"Oh, I know she is." Seth laughed, reaching in the vehicle to give Liz one last deep and passionate kiss. "That should hold you for a while."

He waited until Liz was out of the yard and driving down the road before he climbed into his vehicle and followed her. Their paths diverged as he turned east to Myakka, and Liz headed north to Tampa.

The Alligator Dance

Chapter Eighty-eight

Seth pulled up to the fence surrounding the alligator farm. He parked, squeezing into a spot under some trees, hoping the shade would keep his truck a bit cooler for the day. Stepping out into the heat, he started to sweat right away. It was still early morning, yet the summer temperatures were already in the offensive zone. Walking to the panel by the entrance, Seth punched in the code and waited for the gate to slide open.

The door to Fortier's office was open just enough for Seth to hear raised voices as he approached. Fortier and Dr. Melendez were arguing. Melendez was complaining about not getting paid what Fortier had agreed.

"I should have known better than to go along with this crazy scheme. What about all the money that Boudreaux guy in Louisiana has been paying you?" Melendez raked his hand along the desk, sending an avalanche of papers to the floor.

"It's in a secure account. As soon as the last check clears, you'll get your money. Do you think this place runs on air? Those reptiles must be fed. Workers must be paid, or they quit. I'm the one who is going to end up in prison. It's my name on all the paperwork." Fortier was yelling.

"For God's sake. The eggs have been collected and sold off; you don't need me any more right now. I'm a worker as well, you fucking idiot. You better pay me. Or there might be some anonymous calls to the FWC about this place. And how you do business."

"If my neck is on the line, so is yours," Fortier yelled.

Seth edged closer and rapped on the door.

"Yes, what is it?" Fortier shouted. He didn't want any interruptions and wondered how much Seth had heard. Fortier was worried and had to get Melendez off his back. If the doctor found out he was skimming money into his offshore account in the Caymans, who knows what he might do? His threat to call the FWC agents had him panicking. That was the last thing he wanted. The woman officer had already been around once, and he didn't need closer scrutiny.

Seth stepped into the room. Papers were strewn across the floor. A couple of them showed the alligator ranch's name in Louisiana. If he could only get his hands on those papers.

The Alligator Dance

"What do you want, Seth? Dr. Melendez and I are having a private conversation."

"What do you want me to do today? I can move some gators into different ponds. The hatchlings need more room for where they are now. Or, I can work with Carl on the feeding." Seth didn't want to work with Carl again, but he would if he had to.

"Don't worry about moving the hatchlings. We are going to deliver them to Lousianna this weekend. We'll get $150 for each one. How many do you think are in that pool?"

Seth thought a moment, "Pretty sure, about 80."

"Great, a nice little payday. We can add in some of the larger ones to make up the numbers. They'll pay a bit more for them, too. You and Carl can make the trip on Friday and be back early Sunday."

Driving with Carl back to Lousiana was not what Seth had planned for the weekend. He wanted to take Liz to see his parents, and not be stuck in a truck with ol' misery guts Carl for two days.

Melendez leaned back against a bookcase shaking his head and chuckling. Fortier caught him and said, "What? You want to get paid, right?" Fortier left the office, slamming the door. Carl needed to know about his new plan to move the hatchlings.

Melendez straightened up and looked at Seth, "You do know he's batshit crazy?"

The Alligator Dance

"Why don't you check on the hatchlings and see if they need feeding?" The doctor motioned he was to leave the office and followed Seth out to the shed with the inside pools.

The Alligator Dance

Chapter Eighty-nine

Seth and Melendez walked together to the grow-out shed and stood looking at the two-foot-long gators. "These will have to be moved to a bigger pool soon anyway. We don't have room to keep them, so they have to go," the doctor said. "These can go with the hatchlings on Friday."

"I'll get them some food. I hate to think of these little guys being killed. Just to make boots, wallets, and watch bands and purses," Seth said. "But thanks for the paycheck."

"Think of it this way. They're a product just like a chicken or a cow. It's an industry, and someone has to do it and, in the process, make a profit. And Fortier sure as hell is." Melendez stood and lit another cigar.

"I guess." It still bothered Seth to think about the little guys squirming in the pool in front of him turned into a handbag.

The Alligator Dance

Seth waited until Melendez left. He walked out to the feed shed and ran into Carl. "I need some food for the hatchlings."

Carl gave Seth a dirty look, "I don't have time to deal with them. Take a pail of gator chow. That should hold them for a bit. They won't be around that long."

Seth grabbed one of the slimy five-gallon buckets laying against the wall and filled it with chow. He was thankful he didn't have to chop up smelly chicken bits again.

He carried the chow to the hatchlings. When the reptiles heard him come in and smelled the food, they started chirping and edging closer to the shallow end where they knew their meal would appear. Seth laid out the chow. One after the other, they tossed a nugget down their throat. He had grown fond of the little creatures and hoped he could help shut the farm down soon. What would happen then? Release these sheltered reptiles to the wild? Could they survive? He didn't know. It was too hot to stop and think about all these answers right now.

The Alligator Dance

Chapter Ninety

Putting the bucket aside, Seth decided it was a good a time to get into Fortier's office. He left the shed, trying to think up an excuse for being in his office if he was caught.

He listened at the door. Nothing. He carefully opened the door and found the office empty, and the papers were still scattered across the desk and the floor. He picked up anything with the name of the Louisiana Hightower Ranch and stuffed them in his shirt. Taking a noisy, nervous breath, he retraced his steps back out the door. He collided straight into Carl.

"I thought you were feeding your hatchlings?" Carl looked at Seth with a question on his face and a murderous look in his eyes. "What the hell are you doing here?"

"I finished with the hatchlings. I was... I was going to ask where they wanted the bigger gators moved to," Seth answered.

The Alligator Dance

"How the hell should I know?" Carl roughly pushed past Seth, heading for the office. He heard Carl grumble, "You're the golden boy around here…for now."

The Alligator Dance

Chapter Ninety-one

Seth had to smuggle the papers out of the compound without getting caught. He sprinted to the front gate, alert for Fortier and Melendez. As he punched in the gate code and was waiting for it to slide open, Carl appeared at his elbow. He had followed Seth from the office.

"You're up to something. Now you're out here? You're supposed to be moving those gators to larger pools. Maybe I'll find Mr. Fortier. He might be interested in me finding you heading out the gate and not in the grow-out shed." Carl shoved Seth on the shoulder, spoiling for a fight. Carl outweighed Seth by sixty pounds and was a seasoned brawler.

"Look, Carl, I don't want any trouble. I left my phone in the truck, and I gotta make a call."

"And who is so important?"

The Alligator Dance

"If you must know, it's a sexy little redhead I met in a bar. I want to set something up for after work. She might forget me if I wait too long, and she was really hot and willing. Know what I mean?" Seth was trying to appeal to Carl's baser nature.

"Yeah, I do," Carl smirked. "OK, see if the bimbo has a friend." Carl left laughing to himself. Checking to make sure he had gone, Seth opened his truck and used his pocket knife to slit the worn upholstery under the front seat and wedge the papers in.

Seth hurried back to the shed. His heart sank as he saw Melendez and Fortier waiting for him by a pool.

"Where you been? We need an accurate count on these guys so we can tell Louisianans what to expect," Melendez said. The smoke from their pungent Cuban cigars clouded the air. It added an almost intolerable stench to the stinky, rotten smell from the pools.

"I had to run out for my phone. Hoping for a hot date tonight." Seth figured to keep to the same story in case Carl ratted him out.

Seth watched the two men leave and realized he had been holding his breath. He spent the rest of the day moving the larger alligators from one inside pool to an outside pond. It was not an easy job because these gators were verging on four feet. They fought being manhandled and moved. Grabbing one by the tail, Seth pulled it over the side and onto

The Alligator Dance

the floor. He had to jump on the gator and duck tape its mouth shut without getting bitten. He plopped each flopping reptile onto the flatbed of a four-wheeler. He moved four at a time to the ponds. He was smelly and dripping sweat by the time he moved and released the last of them. Standing up, Seth stretched out the kinks in his back. He stopped to wiggle his fingers in front of his face. Thankfully, he still had all of them.

Fortier came and stood beside him, looking out over the pond, watching the alligators explore their new surroundings, trying to stake out territory. "Good job, Seth. I told Carl that you would be going with him to deliver the hatchlings to the Lousianna ranch. Y'all can leave on Friday."

Seth needed to tell Liz about the sudden plan to move the hatchlings. He hoped she and her team had some idea to shut down the operation before that.

"Sure, Mr. Fortier. I can have them ready to travel that morning."

"Excellent, I counted eighty hatchlings, plus forty of the two-footers. That will be a damn good payday. A great payday, but they gotta make it there alive. I might even give you and Carl a bonus when y'all get back." Fortier left, humming to himself.

The Alligator Dance

Chapter Ninety-two

Liz was in the kitchen, stirring a pot of chili for their supper, when Seth walked in. He came up behind her and, wrapping his arms around her waist, nuzzled her neck.

"Oh no, you don't," Liz said, squirming out of his embrace. "You stink of alligator, swamp, and sweat. Take a shower while the cornbread is baking. Two showers!"

"I guess I do smell a bit."

"Definitely an understatement," Liz said, wrinkling her nose.

"I've got something for you," Seth said, handing her the documents he had stolen from Fortier's office.

As she read, her eyes grew bigger. "You did it." Liz jumped up and gave Seth a strong hug and even stronger kiss, "Ooo, you do stink, but you did it. You found the proof to shut those bastards down. Captain Jacobs can get a team together to raid the farm. Finally, we can get the warrants we need from the judge. I'll call him while you change."

"How soon can we get the warrants? They have a shipment of hatchlings and some larger gators going to Louisiana on Friday, and I'm supposed to go."

"Oh, God, Seth. I'll tell him. Now. Maybe he can speed things up. We have to stop that delivery."

The oven timer sounded. "Oh, damn. I forgot the cornbread." She grabbed a potholder and took it steaming from the oven.

"Get your shower before this gets cold," Liz said, pushing Seth.

When he came back from his shower, Liz was on the phone. She mouthed the words: Captain Jacobs.

Seth sat back and listened to the one-sided conversation. "Yes, I'll bring the papers tomorrow."

"How fast can we get that warrant? They're shipping the hatchlings out the day after tomorrow."

"OK, I'll be at the office first thing. We need to find a friendly judge to issue the search warrant."

Liz spent a few more minutes on the phone but finally hung up full of excitement.

"You heard that. Captain Jacobs is calling in all the favors he can. We will organize a raid on that horrible place sometime tomorrow, early Friday morning at the latest. When are y'all supposed to pull out?"

The Alligator Dance

Liz went to Seth and sat on his lap, laying her head on his muscular, moist chest. "I've been so worried about you working there."

Brushing a stray lock of hair behind Liz's ear, Seth tipped her chin up to look into her eyes.

"I know, I'll be glad to be out of there." He brought his lips down to hers and kissed her gently. "Let's eat that chili of yours and have an early night. We have a tough day ahead of us."

Another summer storm woke them in the middle of the night. Liz clung to Seth, jumping at each crash of thunder. When the alarm went off at 5:00 a.m, neither one wanted to move, but Nokosi was having none of it and demanded they get up.

Liz started the coffee while Seth let the dog out. He stood on the porch, watching Nokosi sniff around before deciding on the perfect stop to lift his leg. The dark sky was clear with a few stars shining and a crescent moon overhead. Ozone fresh air had set off a chorus of croaking tree frogs hiding in the damp foliage. Seth prayed this would be his last day at the Myakka Alligator Farm.

Liz and Seth were both preoccupied with their thoughts as they drove separate directions on their separate missions. Seth worried about the coming raid, but what was uppermost on his mind was Liz. What would happen when

316

this was all over? He wanted her in his life. Had he finally fallen in love? Was Liz feeling the same?

Seth pulled in to the farm parking lot. He wanted to call Liz, hear her voice before he went into the compound to face whatever deadly challenge awaited him.

Liz sat in her truck outside the FWC office. Her mind was racing with the same thoughts as Seth. How would it work out between them—after they arrested these poachers and made the case against them? She had never felt this way before. She loved the security of Seth's arms around her as she slept beside him, hearing his gentle breathing. *Oh, God, I love him. There has to be a future for us.*

The Alligator Dance

Chapter Ninety-three

Carl stood at the gate, waiting for Seth. "Guess what we're doing today?" he laughed.

"Oh, I can't wait," Seth was not in the mood for Carl's feeble attempt at humor.

"We're sorting some of the bull gators for processing. Too many males and not enough females lead to fights. A torn-up hide is not worth anything."

Seth climbed aboard the four-wheeler—hanging on for dear life as Carl drove to the two-acre pond at the back of the property. Seth was positive Carl was trying to toss him off as they arrived in an area that Seth had not seen before. The large pond was surrounded by six-foot high woven rustproof wire fencing stretched over posts driven into the ground eight feet apart. A one by six board was attached to the bottom of the fence on the inside to prevent the alligators from digging their way out to freedom. The wire at the top

The Alligator Dance

was turned inward to keep the alligators inside. They were strong and clever climbers.

"We gotta capture twenty of these guys. These are all bulls and nasty as hell," Carl said, his fingers laced in the fence, watching the fifty or so alligators.

"How the hell are we going to do that?" Seth stood there, watching. Many of the reptiles watched back through mud-encrusted eyes.

"There are feeding stations along the bank. When they come up looking for food, we rope them one at a time. We duck tape up their jaws and wrangle them in the back to those trucks waiting over there," Carl told him, pointing to two pickup trucks parked by a back gate Seth hadn't noticed before.

Carl handed him a catchpole and a roll of black tape. "I'll do one, and then you do the next one."

Seth did not see this as a good idea and watched Carl open the gate. An eight-foot bull alligator approached, growling and hissing. Stretching out the catchpole, Carl looped the rope around the gator's neck and yanked it tight. The reptile went into a desperate roll to get free. The huge creature was rolling clockwise, then counterclockwise. Carl shouted for Seth to open the gate, and he dragged the thrashing reptile through. Seth slammed it behind them. Carl handed the pole to Seth. "Here, take this and keep it tight."

The Alligator Dance

Seth watched, amazed as Carl jumped on the gator's back. Reaching over the snapping jaws, he lifted the bottom jaw, closing its mouth, and wrapped the black tape several times around the jaw and over the eyes. Carl stood up, breathing heavily. He pulled a dirty rag out of his pocket to soak up the sweat from his eyes. He motioned to two men standing by the trucks. "Pick 'em up. Be damn quick about it."

"Now it's your turn," Carl said. Seth thought about how many ways this could go wrong. Opening the gate, Carl said, "Get in there Injun' and catch yourself a big ol' gator." Laughing loudly at some joke only he knew, he pushed Seth toward the gators.

Seth heard the gate slam behind him. He looked back over his shoulder to see Fortier and Mendoza walk up. *Shit. Just what I needed.* Seth thought—*an audience.*

He turned just in time to see a huge bull gator approaching, growling a warning. Two feet away. No time to think. Looping the rope from the catchpole around the reptile's neck, he pulled it tight and backtracked, searching for the gate.

"Hey, open up. Carl, open the gate." Seth shouted in a panic. The gate was not opening, and Carl was laughing.

"Shit, Carl, this ain't funny," Seth struggled to yell.

The gator was rolling in both directions, trying to get loose. Seth's arms felt like they were being torn out of their

The Alligator Dance

sockets. His back was hitting against the gate. Slowly the gate slid open. Dragging the twisting animal into the clear area outside the pond, Seth had no choice but to jump on the bull's back—and try not to get bitten.

The gator was too strong for him and tried to buck him off. Carl climbed on behind Seth to help hold the creature down. Seth reached over the snout and closed its mouth, swiftly wrapping it with black tape.

Breathing heavily, Seth stood and brushed his hands on his jeans. The reptile thrashed its displeasure.

The two men came over to pick up the gator and take him to the truck.

"What the hell were you doing, Carl?" Seth shouted.

"Aw, I was just playing with ya," Carl smirked. The grin on Carl's face told a different story.

Fortier slapped Seth on the back, "I knew you could do it. Wrestling alligators is in your blood. What a show! Carl, I'm going to add a bonus to both your paychecks. Get the rest loaded up." Fortier walked off, humming to himself.

Mendoza took a cigar out of his breast pocket and lit it. The acrid smell competed with the fecund smell of death, rot, and decay in the pond.

Seth hated the smell of their Cuban cigars.

As he turned to catch up with Fortier, he whispered in Seth's ear. "I told you he was crazy," Mendoza said, chuckling as he strolled away. "Batshit crazy!"

The Alligator Dance

Seth and Carl worked for the next few hours in the steaming Florida heat, trapping, wrestling, and taping the rest of the alligators. When they finally slung the last one on the truck, Seth sank to the ground, leaning against the fence. He was exhausted, bruised and smelled vile.

The Alligator Dance

Chapter Ninety-four

Seth laughed, thinking about the reception he would get from Liz when he got home. *Another day I'll have to undress outside.* He pushed up from the ground, every bone in his body aching. He limped to his truck, turned on the engine, and punched up the air.

Seth could be in real danger if the poachers discovered who he was. Too tired to worry about it now, he put the truck in gear and aimed for home. Liz was an hour away, and he had a lot to figure out before then.

Even Nokosi backed away when he stepped out of his truck. Usually, the dog greeted him enthusiastically, but today Nokosi took one sniff, growled softly, and padded back to his spot on the porch.

"OK, so much for the warm welcome home," Seth laughed. He lifted his arm and smelled the rancid odor of alligator excrement, stale pond water, and his own sweat.

"Whew, I don't blame you, dog."

The Alligator Dance

Seth had his hand on the doorknob when Liz yanked the door open, "Oh, no, you don't," she threw him a towel and a bucket. "You know the drill." She stood there, leaning against the doorframe with a wide grin.

Wrapped in the towel, Seth shuffled to a much-needed shower.

"Don't take forever. Supper is almost ready," Liz said, taking the meatloaf out.

Seth crept up behind her as she eased the hot dish on the table. He wrapped his arms around her breasts and kissed the top of her head. Liz leaned back into him, relishing his damp body, warm from the shower. "You smell a hell of a lot better. Eat before it gets cold—meatloaf tonight. No chicken, out of respect for you and the gators! I've got a lot to tell you."

Seth was shoveling mashed potatoes into his mouth. Suddenly Nokosi stood up. He padded to the door, a deep growl, raising the hackles on his back. "What up with you?" Seth asked.

The kitchen window suddenly shattered—showering glass everywhere. "What the hell?" Seth shouted.

Liz screamed and dove under the table, grabbing Nokosi. Seth jumped up and spotted a light-colored pickup truck speeding down the road, a plume of dust in its wake. A large rock with a note wrapped around it lay amid the glass.

The Alligator Dance

"This guy has gone old school to deliver his messages." Seth unwrapped the note and read it out loud. "Stay away from the alligator farm if you know what's good for you."

"Is this for you or me?" Liz asked.

"It was not Carl's truck, so I don't know for sure. Someone could have found out you are still staying here. Oh, God, Liz, I just don't know." Seth hugged her tight, kissing her forehead tenderly. "Let's clean up this mess before one of us gets cut."

Liz took the dog and put him in the bedroom while they swept up. They checked their dinner for any stray glass pieces.

Seth sat and waited for Liz to let Nokosi out. She said, "Somehow, I knew this supper would get cold. Do you want me to reheat it?"

"No, I'm too hungry. It's perfect." Seth helped himself to another slice of meatloaf.

"You have no idea who's behind that note?"

"If Stan weren't in jail, I'd say it was him. I think it was one of Fortier's workers. He's worried the FWC is getting too nosy and wants you to back off. Again."

"The other day, when I went to check the Gator Hollow, I heard voices. Pretty sure one of the voices was Stan. Another thing I'm sure of is that he put that rattler in your truck and cut up the raccoon on the hood, too. It was all to scare you off investigating the farm." Seth leaned back in his chair, finishing off his iced tea.

"Well, he got that wrong," Liz said, standing to clear the table. "What are you going to do about Stan?"

"I'll let Captain Jacobs decide his fate. As far as I'm concerned, his career as a park ranger is over. The District Attorney may have some charges and jail time in store for him as well."

The Alligator Dance

Chapter Ninety–five

Seth let Nokisi out to do his business, stopping in the doorway to watch the stars fade as the sun rose in the purple Southwest Florida sky. The air hung thick and sweet after tropical rain during the night. Liz slipped up behind, encircling him with her arms and laying her head on his back, inhaling his musky sleep aroma.

"I wish you'd skip the farm. Stay out of this, in case it goes wrong," Liz whispered. "I'm going crazy worrying about you every time you go out there."

"If I don't go, they'll ship those alligator youngsters off to Louisiana anyway. They have it scheduled for today. Carl would like anyone but me to ride with him. It's a long way, and he speaks two dozen words."

"Keep your head down when we come knocking. Captain Jacobs has a team ready to go. Maybe a dozen officers or more ready and waiting; we had a briefing yesterday."

"Don't I get to worry about you, too?" Seth twisted around to take Liz in his arms, his head resting against hers.

"I'm happy you do, but I'll be fine. I carry my Glock .45 and wear my flak vest. Feel naked without 'em."

"OK, we'll get to worry about each other." Seth held Liz at arm's length and looked into her eyes.

"What are you doing?"

"After this is all over, we need to talk about things."

"Like what, my handsome Seminole brave?" Liz knew what he was talking about and gave him a coy smile. He melted like butter on grits.

"Look, I love you, baby, and think you love me. Just not sure what we're going to do about it."

"Let's wait until today is over and go from there."

Seth drew her in and captured her lips, kissing her deep and passionately. She smelled like honey and tasted like orange juice. She responded, making him hurt in ways he didn't think possible. He wanted to take her back to bed, but that would have to wait.

Breaking away, Seth said, "Let's get this done." He held her hand while walking to their vehicles.

"See you later, Chief! Be careful. Always." Liz reached up and brushed at the stray lock of raven black hair covering Seth's gray-green eyes. She kissed him gently before getting into her FWC truck.

Seth watched her drive away. He mouthed a silent prayer again to the Creator God of the Seminoles, Breathmaker, for her safety. Lately, Seth had done a lot of praying for help and guidance from his ancestors. He hoped they would answer soon.

Seth jumped in his truck and drove a nervous half-hour down the back roads to the alligator farm in Myakka.

The Alligator Dance

Chapter Ninety-six

Keying in the code, he waited in the heat for the rusty gate to slide open, dragging his damp arm across his forehead, salty sweat burning his eyes. Both hands trembled. Stepping inside, he took a moment to calm himself. Whatever happened today might change his life forever.

He walked to the grow-out shed where they raised the hatchlings until they were big enough to graduate into one of the ponds. He watched the little reptiles splashing around in the three pools. Hissing, pushing, and shoving, piling on. Just like kids on a playground.

Carl banged the door open, startling Seth as he watched the little guys scrambling over each other. "Come on, let's get these critters loaded. I want to be on the road before the traffic starts."

The Alligator Dance

Seth had to stall. He couldn't let Carl ship this lot out to Lousiana. He hoped Liz and the FWC officers would converge soon.

"Yeah, sure. What are we putting the hatchlings in?"

"There's containers in the damn storage shed." Carl walked away, shaking his head. The radio on his belt buzzed to announce someone at the entrance. "Can I help you?" he growled.

Slapping the radio back on his belt, he stormed out the door. "Crap, just what we need. That bitch from the FWC is back. Grab the containers from the shed and load up, Tonto! Get your red Indian ass moving."

Seth remembered to breathe, grasping the edge of the pool. "I think my prayers have been answered, and you might have just gotten pardoned." He smiled at himself for talking to the baby alligators. They were cute in an ugly and dangerous sort of way. Seth longed to see them swimming free in one of the local rivers and lakes where they belonged.

Seth did his best to look busy, so he went for the containers, loading them on a 4x4 with a trailer attached. He drove it back in low gear and began to unload. Easy does it. Slowly.

Carl didn't want to let Liz into the compound, but she waved a search warrant.

"What are you doing back here, bitch? You saw it all the first time around."

The Alligator Dance

"This is a legal search warrant, and you are obliged to let us in," Liz shouted as Carl tried to close the gate, preventing her from entering.

Liz blocked the gate from closing with her hip and boot. "This is not your lucky day. I have a job to do, and I'm going to do it whether you like it or not."

Liz stealthily pressed a button on her phone. A few seconds later, sirens rang out. Three FWC vans raced into the parking area, blue lights ablaze. Carl tried to shove Liz out of the way to close the gate and keep the officers out.

Liz shoved back. Carl tripped over his own feet, landing hard in a rain puddle. Liz forced the gate all the way to allow the captain's cruiser inside. The rest of the camo-clad team followed on foot, weapons drawn, Glock pistols, MAC-10s, shotguns, batons, pepper spray at the ready. They wore helmets, vests, body armor, and shields. They were a formidable assault team.

Jacobs handed her a helmet and a flak vest. Two officers guarded the gate. Walking through the compound, the team rounded up Hector, Manuel, and a couple of others. They had been hanging around waiting to move some more of the bigger alligators for processing. The men tried to run—hiding behind the buildings. They were found or ran straight into FWC officers as they fanned out around the compound.

The Alligator Dance

"We didn't do nothin'," Manuel yelled, trying to twist free. "Let go of me."

Hector hung his head resigned. "Do you turn me over to ICE?"

"Sorry, man, I can't answer that. It's up to the DA." A young officer answered him.

Liz led the way to Fortier's office. Captain Jacobs didn't bother to knock, pushing the door open. Fortier and Melendez were at the desk going over the books. Jacobs heard Melendez ask, "How much did you say?"

Fortier looked at the FWC officers in shock as they entered his office.

"What? Who are you? Get the hell out. Immediately." Fortier ranted, smoke from his cheroot circling his head. Melendez slunk back against the wall hoping to be invisible, inching his way to the door.

"Oh no, you don't." Liz drew her handgun and pointed it at Melendez to drive home her command.

"Etienne Fortier, you are under arrest for illegally trespassing on state-owned property, for taking state property, and the transporting of the said property across state lines. Namely alligators and eggs. There will also be charges of tax evasion and RICO charges." He then recited the Miranda warning to both Fortier and Melendez.

"This is outrageous. Do you know who I am? I employ people who can't get jobs elsewhere." Fortier was indignant and puffing himself up. "I'm important to the economy of this area."

"Yeah, we'll see about that. I suggest you shut up. Put your hands behind your back," Jacobs told Fortier.

"You, too," Liz dangled her cuffs in front of Melendez. Resigned to his fate, Melendez turned around and let Liz proceed to cuff him.

Jacobs took his attention off Fortier to check on Liz. "You alright with him over there?" In that split second, Fortier twisted out of the captain's grasp, shoving him into the desk. Jacobs tripped over a chair and thudded to the floor. Liz had her hands full with Melendez.

"Get after him. Melendez, don't you friggin' move," Jacobs shouted, standing and drawing his weapon to cover the doctor. He clicked on his radio to alert the team outside.

"Fortier is out there on the run. Cut him off," Jacobs ordered. "Curtis, come take Melendez off my hands."

Liz hurtled out the door, chasing Fortier. The slippery Cajun hurtled out the door, handcuffs dangling from one of his wrists. He ran awkwardly to the ponds. His slick designer boots slipping and sliding on the muddy, mossy path. Trucks loaded with alligators idled at the back gate, their drivers under the care of the FWC officers.

Seth heard the commotion and hurried out of the grow shed to see Fortier racing away with Liz in hot pursuit, maybe ten yards behind.

The Alligator Dance

"Fortier, stop," Liz shouted. "There is no place to run."

Seth ran to intercept the fleeing man. Fortier was throwing punches and shaking Seth to release his grip. They crashed into Liz, causing her to lose her balance and topple over a short fence, sliding down an embankment into the pond with hungry alligators waiting below.

Liz lay there, stunned, blood seeping from a gash on her head from hitting a rock. She had landed in a holding pen for some of the largest gators.

Seth's heart dropped. He threw a punch, hitting Fortier with everything he had. The force sent the Cajun crashing to the ground. Fortier looked like he was out cold. Blood streamed from his nose and scalp where he'd hit the ground.

Three gators slithered toward Liz as she lay on the pen deck. "Shit. Liz, Liz," Seth called, jumping over the fence and dropping down beside her.

"Liz, come on, girl, or you'll be an alligator's dinner." Seth watched, terrified, as an aggressive ten-foot bull alligator inched towards them.

Liz opened her eyes, "Seth?" she smiled, not realizing the danger until she heard the threat coming towards them. "Oh, crap." The alligator approached— growling, hissing, its jaws open, ready to bite. Seth yanked her to her feet and gave her a boost.

The Alligator Dance

"Liz, grab the top of the fence. Pull yourself up." Once up, she reached down to help Seth.

Fortier, still groggy from the punch, stood up and threw Liz out of the way and to the ground. He tried to pry Seth's fingers from the top of the fence rail. Seth reached up and grabbed Fortier's wrist and hauled him over and down to the wet, muddy ground of the pond, right into the waiting jaws of the bull alligator.

They heard the scream as he helped Liz to stand. They watched as the alligator latched onto Fortier's right thigh, dragging him further into the pond. Then, the death roll.

Liz buried her face in Seth's chest, trying to block out the blood-curdling screams. Two more alligators argued over Fortier. He didn't have a chance, as they fought and tore him apart.

Captain Jacobs walked up to see the alligators retreating with their prize. "Oh, God, is that Fortier?"

"It was," Seth answered.

"You two OK?"

"Yes, sir, we are." Seth and Liz, both bloody and bruised, echoed.

Liz wiped the mud, blood, and tears from her cheeks and eyes. "I never want to see anything like that ever again."

"No man should die like that," said Seth. "No matter what they have done."

The Alligator Dance

The captain gave Liz an awkward hug. Then he returned to business. "We have everyone in custody. Melendez is telling quite a story. Of course, he's blaming the whole scheme on Etienne Fortier."

"How about Hector and those other poor guys? They were only trying to make a living. What's going to happen to them?" Seth asked. He had taken a liking to the old Hispanic man he had rescued after a snake bite.

"Six are restrained in the van. The DA will have to take a look and see what charges might come their way," Jacobs said. "I'm sure there will be some and a bit of jail time. It depends on the judge."

Officer Curtis came jogging up, "Hey, where is that guy Fortier? I thought you'd have him in cuffs by now."

Jacobs tipped his head to the pond. Curtis approached the fence and looked over. He quickly turned away, covering his mouth, retching. Racing to the side of the nearest shed, he lost his banana and cornflake breakfast. Laying there, bobbing at the edge of the green sludge pool, was Fortier's severed left hand attached to a handcuff. An expensive Rolex on the wrist, still keeping perfect time.

"Seth, can you get that out of there? We'll need it for the coroner, and maybe evidence," Jacobs said.

Seth came back with a long pole with a hook. Stretching over the fence, he hooked the hand by the cuffs and slowly brought it up. Fortier's watch was intact and his gold and onyx signet ring emblazoned with a fleur-de-lis still on his little finger. The captain bagged the remains in an evidence bag. He'd worked a lot of death scenes, and this was among the worst.

Curtis returned, looking very green, like his drab uniform. "Curtis, grow a pair, will ya? Take this and book it into evidence," Jacobs told the young officer. He took the bag, holding it at arm's length. He was getting greener by the moment. He ducked behind another shed and reappeared a couple of minutes later.

"Is he going to be alright?" Liz asked, feeling sorry.

"He's young. He'll see worse. Seth, I have to thank you for your part in this operation."

"I kind of had to." Seth smiled, looking down at Liz. He had his arm around her shoulder. Her eyes were red and slightly swollen, still wet from crying, face smudged, uniform wet with gator stink. Seth knew it would take them both a long time to get over seeing Etienne Fortier ravaged and eaten by alligators.

"What's going to happen to all these guys?" Seth asked Jacobs, nodding to the gators.

"The FWC will come in and feed them until they can be relocated."

"Some of them came from my park. Could I take some of the hatchlings back to where they belong?"

338

The Alligator Dance

"That should be OK. Speaking of paperwork, I need both of you to write a statement about what happened here with Fortier. It looks like he got what he deserved. Proud of you both. Hose off somewhere around here. Go home for now, and I'll see you in my office early Monday morning."

Seth helped Liz take off her bulletproof vest, handing it to Jacobs. "We'll be there." Seth shook the captain's hand.

"You've got a good man there," Jacobs said to Liz.

"Yeah, I do." Liz leaned into Seth—his arms around her shoulders as they walked out of the Myakka Alligator Farm.

The Alligator Dance

Chapter Ninety–seven

"I'm so glad that's over."

"Oh, yuck… Do I stink as bad as you do?"

"I wasn't going to say anything, but yeah, you do."

"I'll race you to the shower. The first one there gets to wash off the other," Liz laughed, taking off down the hall.

Seth cursed as he heard his cell phone ring. Looking at the readout, he saw it was his father.

He showed the display to Liz. "Let me take this." Seth walked out onto the porch and sat in a rocker. The evenings were steamy, and the cicadas were buzzing away in the trees.

"Hi, Dad, what's up?"

"You're mom has been nagging me to have you bring your friend Liz back for a visit. There's a dance at the community center tomorrow. Any chance you could make it? She's driving me crazy."

The Alligator Dance

"I'll ask Liz." Seth hesitated before continuing. "Dad, how did you know that Mom was the one for you?"

"That's a loaded question. You thinking in that direction with Liz?"

"Yeah, maybe, but we've only known each other a few weeks."

"I have an idea that might help. Come up tomorrow, and we'll talk. Please don't say anything about this to your mom, or she will be inviting all the cousins to a wedding before the sun rises the next day."

Seth chuckled, knowing his dad was probably right. "I'll call you."

Seth hung up and, stripping quickly, surprised Liz when he stepped in the shower behind her. He held her and let the warm water spill over them. Liz let her mind drift to how she wished this moment would last forever. The feel of their slick bodies against each other was magic. The stress of their day was slowly fading.

The sound of Nokosi pacing and whining interrupted them, "Shit, what now?" A loud knock on the door had the dog running to the kitchen.

"Better go see who it is. Be careful." Liz said, reaching for a towel to wrap around herself. Seth covered up and went to the door.

Liz heard Seth say, "What the hell are you doing here?"

The Alligator Dance

Darrell stood in the glow from the porch light with his girlfriend, Marcia, holding a couple of plastic grocery bags, "That's no way to welcome someone who is bringing steaks and wine."

"Did I forget something?" Seth was perplexed. He'd planned a quiet evening alone with Liz, but such was life.

"No, I just figured that if I waited for a proper invite, I'd never get one. You got any idea why two FWC officers would come around asking questions about Stan's activities over the last few weeks?" Darrell asked, "What have you been up to, Chief?"

Come on in then. Make yourself at home while I get dressed." Seth passed Liz in the hallway.

"Sorry, we have guests," Seth kissed Liz lightly on the cheek.

"It's OK. We have all night." Liz winked.

God, how much he loved Liz. She could read his thoughts.

Liz walked into the kitchen to see Darrell and a young woman preparing a meal.

"Hi Liz, this is my girlfriend, Marcia."

"Marcia, meet Florida Wildlife Conservation Officer Liz Corday."

Liz stepped around the table and shook hands. "Hi, call me Liz."

The Alligator Dance

"Nice to meet you, Liz. Sorry about turning up like this," Marcia apologized. "Darrell just wouldn't let it rest when the FWC came around today."

"It's fine. I guess you brought dinner in that bag. That's great. We've had a rough day." Liz pulled a chair out and sat down at the table. She was going to take full advantage of someone else cooking.

"Are you OK? You look like you got a nasty cut on your head." Marcia asked.

"I guess I did. It's part of a long story." Liz pulled out a couple of bottles of Seth's wine, and placed glasses on the table.

"Yeah, about that?" Darrel asked, turning away from chopping the salad he was working on. "Two of your guys were asking questions about Stan being involved with poachers. You and Seth have anything to do with that?"

Darrell ducked as Seth threw a wet towel at his head. "Hey, Chief. It seems you had a busy day. Care to enlighten us?"

"How about we get those steaks going? I'll tell you all about it over a glass of nice wine," Seth said, showing Darrell the grill on the back porch.

Gathered around the kitchen table, Seth and Liz filled Darrell and Marcia in.

"You know the beginning," Seth said. "Those egg poachers were targeting the park."

The Alligator Dance

"That's right. Stan was supposed to be monitoring Gator Hollow," Darrell said, filling his wine glass again.

"Well, it turns out Stan was working with the poachers. Feeding them information on Liz and how she was staying at my place."

"How did he know?"

"Maybe he heard you on the phone and put two and two together."

"Now that I think about it, he was on his cell phone a lot. I thought his wife had him on a short leash," Darrell laughed.

"He was trying to frighten me off. He put a rattlesnake in my truck," Liz said.

Marcia shuddered. "Oh my God. How awful."

"Stan's next trick was to leave me a slaughtered raccoon on the hood. When the poachers figured we were getting too close, someone threw a rock through the kitchen window with a note to stay away from the alligator farm in Myakka."

"Wait, you said *we*," Darrell said, straightening up in his chair, looking very curious. "You're not telling the whole story."

Seth got up to open another bottle of wine. "There never was a wedding at the Big Cypress Rez. I was working undercover for the FWC."

The Alligator Dance

"You what?" Darrell choked on his wine. "You've got to be kidding me."

"I had to pretend I needed a job so I could get hired at the gator farm. I've been gathering evidence to put these guys away."

"You're one crazy Indian."

"You don't know the half of it." Liz reached out for Seth's hand.

"I'm guessing there's more going on here than catching bad guys," Marcia said, eyes wide with curiosity. Her feminine intuition was working overtime. She'd explain it to Darrell later.

"We're still figuring that one out," Liz and Seth said together, setting off everyone laughing.

All their questions answered, Darrell and Marcia helped with the cleanup and said their goodbyes. Seth walked the young couple out to Darrell's truck. "I'll be back next week. We'll let Dan Myers replace Stan for as long as he's able. I've got a couple of things to do."

"Will do. Come back soon. I want to hear all the details you left out this evening. And knowing you, I bet there are some good ones."

Liz and Marcia hugged while Seth clapped Darrell on the back. "I'll probably need some time off again if this goes to trial."

"We'll figure it out if that happens," Darrell said.

The Alligator Dance

Chapter Ninety-eight

Later sitting on the couch, relaxing in each other's arms, watching an old movie, Seth broke the silence. "I still think there will be a trial for Melendez and his crowd. We'll have to be there unless they plead guilty straightaway."

"Right." Liz pulled away. *Would this be the end of her relationship with Seth? What was her relationship, and was it going anywhere?* She had fallen in love with her Seminole warrior.

"Seth," Liz walked away to stand in front of the fireplace in the sitting area. She bit her lip nervously and continued. "We have something to talk about. I need to know how you feel about *us*."

Seth rushed to her, taking her hands in his. "I want there always to be an *us*." Raising her hands, he kissed them gently. "In case you haven't figured it out by now, I love you, Officer Liz Corday. I want you in my life today. And always."

"That's good because I feel the same way." Liz leaned in to take his lips with hers. Letting her heart win was a big step for Liz. Her last relationship had ended badly with deceit and betrayal. Loving and trusting again was hard.

Seth released her hands and drew her closer, kissing her deeply, hoping to convey how he felt about her. He reveled in the feel of her body against his, bringing in the smell of her raspberry shampoo. But there was more to it. He loved her heart, determination, kindness, and so much more.

The Alligator Dance

Chapter Ninety-nine

In the morning, cleaning up after breakfast, Seth told Liz of the invitation from his parents. "I thought it might be a nice change from chasing poachers."

"Only if I can wear something like your mother had on last time. Do they sell those clothes on the rez?"

"I think so. We can go up early and see what we can find."

Liz and Seth busied themselves around the house for a couple of hours before setting off for Tampa and the Seminole Reservation.

They took their time shopping and arrived at his parents' house in plenty of time to visit before the dance.

"Oh, don't you look wonderful," Seth's mother said as she opened the door to their mobile home. Liz beamed with excitement and twirled, showing off her new shirt in the

The Alligator Dance

colorful patchwork style of the Seminoles. Rowena was so pleased to see her son with Liz. She silently hoped that Seth would finally settle down with Liz and give her the grandchildren she could boast about to the other women. She was tired of everyone asking if Seth was married yet. Rowena wanted to pass around her pictures of her grandchildren like the other women at the community center.

"Andres, come greet your son and Liz," Rowena called. "Come in. I have a nice supper for you before the dance."

"Thanks, Mom, but you didn't have to go to a lot of trouble for us."

"Don't tell her that. She's been cooking all day for you," Andres said, stepping into the room and embracing his son and giving Liz a warm smile. Andres was conflicted about his son not choosing a Seminole woman. Tradition and the Seminole culture were important to him, but he knew times were changing, and Seth had chosen to make his living off the reservation, and he must accept that.

"How often do I have my only son come for a meal with his parents?" Rowena said, stepping up to gently pat Seth on the cheek. "Maybe you will come more often if I feed you."

"Come sit down. We will talk and eat." Rowena put dishes on the table that were filled with incredible smelling grilled chicken, and from her garden, green beans, thickly sliced tomatoes, and cucumbers.

"Do you remember this, Seth?" Rowena asked as she placed a bowl in front of Seth.

Seth lifted the bowl and smelled. He dipped his spoon in and tasted. Wide-eyed with wonder, he asked, "Is this the special sauce Uncle Zackery makes down on the Big Cypress Rez?"

"Yes, that is Uncle Zackery's Golden Sauce. We had him send us a couple of jars. We hope now you will visit us more often," Rowena said.

"It's a bribe," Andres laughed. Smiling, he reached out to hold his wife's hand.

After dinner, Seth pushed himself away from the table. "I can't eat another bite."

"Me either," Liz said. "I haven't had fresh from the garden vegetables in a long time. That was incredible. Can I help you clean up?"

"Yes, we will let Seth and Andres go and talk before the dance."

"Guess that's our cue to get out of the way. Let's sit on the screened porch." Andres led the way to the small area off the main room and opened the sliding door. It was a warm night but not that bad after he turned on the overhead fan.

After getting comfortable, Andres asked Seth, "So what did you want to talk to me about?"

The Alligator Dance

Seth was embarrassed talking about his love life with his father, but he needed the older man's wisdom.

Taking a deep breath, he plunged ahead. "Dad, I love Liz, yet I don't know what to do about it."

"You have only known each other for a short time. Are you thinking about asking Liz to marry you?"

"That's the problem. I don't know if I want to get married. At least not yet. It's a big step. I want Liz in my life, but as you say, we have not known each other that long."

"I met your mother when we were still teenagers. I fell in love with her straightaway, but we were too young. Back then, a young couple would agree to go steady."

"What's going steady?"

"It's an old custom from the 1950s. I don't think young people know about it anymore. A dating couple would agree that they would only date each other and see where it went. That gave your mom and me time to get to know each other and decide if we would marry or not. Lucky for me, we stayed together and were married right there on Big Cypress with all the family present. That is what I want for you."

"OK, does the couple just shake hands or what?"

"Usually, the boy would give the girl his high school ring or something like that. She would wear the symbol on a chain around her neck for all to see that she was taken."

"I don't have a ring."

The Alligator Dance

"I have that figured out." Andres dug in his shirt pocket and pulled out a silver chain. On the chain was a beautifully carved snake in silver. "We are of the snake clan. Liz does not have a clan. We will bring her into ours if she wishes. It is allowed that we do this."

"Dad, I don't know what to say." Seth was getting emotional. *This might be the perfect answer. Now all he had to do was ask Liz.*

The Alligator Dance

Chapter One Hundred

Walking into the community center that evening was more relaxed than before, but Seth did look for Helen and her brother. He hoped there would not be another scene like the last time. They all sat with Mina and Georgia again and enjoyed the dancing and the music.

Excusing himself, he nodded to his father. "Come outside," Seth took Liz's hand and guided her through the crowd to the back of the community center. "It's getting a bit warm in there."

Seth found a seat on a worn bench under an old Brazilian pepper tree and pulled Liz down beside him. "Remember, we said we had to talk about where we would take whatever was going on between us after we caught the poachers."

The Alligator Dance

"Yeah. I remember," Liz answered cautiously, her heart pounding. This conversation could go either way.

"Well, my dad told me about this custom from the old days that if two people want to be together but are not ready to be engaged or get married, they can agree to go steady."

"OK. I'm with you so far."

"The girl wears a school ring or other emblem from the guy. I'm from the snake clan. Dad gave me this." Seth held out the beautifully carved silver snake pendant on an eighteen-inch silver chain.

"Oh, Seth, it's lovely." Liz took it gently in her hands.

"So, will you go steady with me?"

"Yes, yes, of course." Liz's face lit up with joy. "Will you put it on for me?" Liz handed the necklace to Seth and turned her back to him. He lifted her sandy hair and fastened the chain around her neck, and kissed the clasp. Seth took her in his arms, "Until we take the next step." He kissed her, drawing her into him, feeling her body respond to his. Breathless, they broke apart.

The Alligator Dance

Chapter One Hundred-one

Walking back into the dance holding hands, Seth and Liz stopped at his parents' table. His father wore a huge grin, and Rowena gasped and brought her hands to her chest.

"Mom, don't go booking the preacher yet."

"My son, I'm so happy. Liz, you are so perfect for him. You are already family to us." Rowena beamed.

"You two better get going, or she'll be sending out the invitations," Andres laughed. Rowena slapped him on the arm, laughing.

"Mom, when and if Liz and I decide to get married, you will be the first person to find out."

Seth took Liz by the hand and guided her through the crowd. Holding hands, lost in thought for a few minutes. Stopping under a street lamp, Seth spun Liz around, "I've been doing some thinking, what's it take to be an FWC officer? Would they let us work together?"

"Wow, I can get you some information. Captain Jacobs will be happy to help you."

The Alligator Dance

"I guess that answers some of the *where are we going from here* questions. I love you, Liz."

"I love you too." Liz threw her arms around his neck and brought him to her, finding his lips with hers and kissed him. He was stirring sensations traveling deep inside her.

From up on the porch of the mobile home across the road, a man shouted, "Hey, ain't you two found a room yet?"

The Alligator Dance

The Alligator Dance

The Florida Fish and Wildlife Conservation Commission

The Law Enforcement Officers of the Florida Fish and Wildlife Conservation Commission have full police powers and statewide jurisdiction. They patrol rural, wilderness and inshore and offshore areas and are often the sole law enforcement presence in many remote parts of the state. The Division of Law Enforcement has cooperative agreements with the National Marine Fisheries Service and the U.S. Fish and Wildlife Service. Officers are also cross-deputized to enforce federal marine fisheries and wildlife laws, thus ensuring state and federal consistency in resource-protection efforts. (Taken from the FWC website)

For more information on the work of the FWC
https://myfwc.com/about/inside-fwc/le/what-we-do

Please support their mission and visit FWC Officer Frank Robb's website

https://eearss.org/

@AlligatorRobb

The Alligator Dance

The Alligator Dance

About the Author

Brenda M. Spalding is a prolific award-winning author with several children's books and romantic suspense novels for adults.

Originally from Newton, Massachusetts, she settled in Bradenton, Florida, with her husband after returning from the military. The author has two children and one grandson.

She is a past president of the National League of American Pen Women - Sarasota branch, a member of the Sarasota Authors Connection, Sarasota fiction Writers, Florida Authors and Publishers, Florida Writers Association and a co-founding member and current president of ABC Books Inc. A 501c3 writers' organization in Sarasota Florida.

If you enjoyed this book, please leave a review. Authors count on their readers for review more than you know. You can contact the author at
spaldingauthor@gmail.com